CBT SKILLS FOR TEENS

How to Manage Anxiety, Build Confidence, Navigate Big Emotions and Thrive in a Stressful, Ever-Changing World

Emma Davis

Impact
PUBLISHING

You can train your mind to feel stronger and lighter.

Welcome to a Brand New Adventure!

We are delighted to bring this book to you! Crafted for teens, it's here to **support, inspire,** and **make learning exciting**.

Engaging and packed with value, it breaks down essential life topics in a way that's **simple, meaningful, and empowering**.

What Makes This Book Special?

- Visuals that make lessons pop.
- Tips and takeaways to use right away.
- Quick activities to practice as you go.
- One chapter at a time, perfect for weekly reading.

TABLE OF CONTENTS

Quick Favor!

Your Review Makes a Difference

If you enjoy this book, please leave a review at
emmadavisbooks.com
or
Amazon.com

SCAN ME

Your review helps us guide teens in the art of living—and gives parents the peace of mind they deserve.

Page Left Blank Intentionally

INTRODUCTION

"Once you learn to think differently, you start to feel differently."

— Dr. David D. Burns, Feeling Good: The New Mood Therapy

I REMEMBER THE FIRST time I saw the shift happen. It was during a Tuesday afternoon session, the kind where the air is thick not because of tension but because something important is about to happen, though nobody knows it yet.

Jasmine, a 14-year-old I'd been seeing for about six weeks, sat across from me. She was quiet, guarded, her eyes flicking between the clock and the window more often than they met mine. That had been her pattern. She came in with a weight that didn't belong to someone her age; overwhelmed by school, tangled up in social anxiety, and carrying around a belief that her thoughts were facts, that her worst fears about herself must be true because they felt so real.

What stood out about Jasmine wasn't how sad or anxious she seemed but how deeply convinced she was that things couldn't change. She told me, without any hesitation, "I'm just the kind of person who fails at stuff. That's just who I am." Not "how I feel" but who she was. And in that one sentence, I heard what CBT calls a cognitive distortion, a pattern of thinking that tricks us into accepting unhelpful beliefs as truths.

In that session, I asked her to try something different. We didn't dive into feelings right away. Instead, we grabbed a whiteboard and mapped out what happened the last time she "failed" a group presentation at school. We broke it into parts: What actually happened? What did she think? What did she feel? And what did she do afterward?

As she walked through it, something changed. She started to notice that her thoughts, like "I ruined it for everyone," didn't match the facts. The group got a decent grade. Her teacher said she did fine. One classmate even thanked her for helping with the slides. Jasmine paused. Then she said something small but unforgettable: "So... maybe I wasn't as bad as I thought."

That was the turning point.

From there, we began using core CBT tools: identifying thinking traps, learning to challenge automatic thoughts, and experimenting with new behaviors. Over time, Jasmine didn't just feel better, but she also thought differently. She understood that thoughts can seem true even when they are not. That single realization gave her something many teens don't realize they have: the ability to change how they relate to their thoughts.

I've seen moments like that again and again. CBT doesn't promise an instant fix, but it gives teens a framework they can actually use, a way to understand themselves without shame, and to make changes that feel manageable.

This book is for young people like Jasmine. It's built on proven CBT techniques and grounded in real-world experience. Whether you're dealing with anxiety, low mood, stress, or self-doubt, CBT has something practical to offer, and that's what this journey is about.

Fun Fact

Teens feel emotions more intensely than adults because the emotional part of the brain (amygdala) develops faster than the thinking part (prefrontal cortex). That's why strong feelings can hit hard, and why learning to understand them helps a lot.

📕 Why This Book Exists

What Jasmine experienced isn't unique, but the tools that helped her aren't always easy to access, especially for teens. That's why this book was written.

🌱 Why Teens Deserve Direct Support

The goal is simple: to offer a supportive, easy-to-follow guide for teens who are feeling overwhelmed by their thoughts and emotions, and for the parents, caregivers, or professionals who want to walk alongside them with care. It's not meant to replace therapy but to be a helpful companion. A book you can return to when you feel stuck. A place to learn how CBT works in real life, not just as a theory, but as something you can apply to your day, your stress, your social anxiety, your school pressure.

CBT (Cognitive Behavioral Therapy) is one of the most researched and recommended approaches for dealing with common teen mental health issues like anxiety, depression, and low self-esteem. What sets it apart is that it doesn't just tell you *what* you're feeling; it helps you understand *why* and gives you ways to challenge unhelpful thoughts and test out new behaviors. It's built on the idea that your thoughts, feelings, and actions are connected and that if you can adjust one, you can shift the others too.

🛠️ How This Book Will Help You Use CBT

Each chapter will break down a specific topic or challenge that teens commonly face. You're not expected to have all the answers before you start. This book is here to meet you wherever you are, whether you're just starting to notice something feels off or you've been struggling for a while. It's okay to take things one page at a time. CBT doesn't demand perfection. It invites curiosity and gives you space to figure things out without judgment. You'll find examples, brief exercises, helpful check-ins, and ideas you can try on your own or with support. The approach is direct, grounded in science, and shaped by real conversations I've had in therapy rooms over the years.

The main aim? To show that mental health isn't just something that happens *to* you. It's something you can work on, with the right tools, support, and understanding.

Who This Book Is For

Let's be clear: this book is for teens. Not adults who think like teens. Not professionals pretending to speak the teen language. It's for actual teenagers; people trying to figure out how to deal with pressure, weird moods, social stuff, overthinking, and all the other things that can make everyday life harder than it should be.

It's for the teen who keeps getting stuck in their own head. The one who's tired of being told to "calm down" when calming down isn't that simple. It's for the teen who finds themselves overthinking a single text, replaying moments from school, or lying in bed feeling like everything's too much but not knowing how to explain it.

This book also shows that not everyone who needs help wants to sit in an office and talk for an hour. Or maybe therapy isn't an option right now for a bunch of reasons. That's why this book exists: to offer something solid that teens can pick up when they need to understand what's going on inside and how to deal with it in a way that doesn't feel like it's written for someone else.

Even though this book is written with teens in mind, others will learn something too, like parents who want to help without making things worse or teachers trying to support a student who's struggling. But first and foremost, this is *your* book. If you're a teen who wants to understand your mind better and feel more in control, you're in the right place.

What Makes This Book Different

There are plenty of books out there about mental health. Some are filled with theories, some are packed with advice from adults who mean well, and some sound like they were written in another language altogether. This one is different, and that's on purpose.

For starters, it talks *to* teens, not about them. The language used here is straight-up, real, and easy to understand. No fluff. No complicated explanations. Just clear ideas that make sense when you're in the middle of something hard and need a way through it.

But more importantly, this isn't just something to read. It's something to *use*. Every chapter includes interactive exercises, not the boring kind that feels like homework, but things that actually help. Things like filling in thought loops, mapping out moods, and trying out different ways of reacting to stuff that usually sets you off. The book becomes a kind of toolkit you can carry with you. Open a page, try something, and see what happens.

It also gets that not every teen comes from the same background or sees the world in the same way. That's why the examples in this book don't follow just one type of story. You'll find situations that reflect all sorts of experiences: different cultures, different family setups, different kinds of pressure. Whether you're juggling expectations at school, figuring out friendships, or dealing with things that no one else seems to understand, there's something here that fits.

The goal isn't to tell you what's wrong with you. It's to help you figure out what's been going on *for* you and what you can do about it. This book is about giving teens a way to take small steps forward without pretending that everything's perfect. It's honest. It's useful. And it was made with real life in mind.

What You'll Get Out of This Book

This isn't a book about "just think positive" or "take a deep breath and move on." It's about real tools for real situations, especially the messy ones.

By the end, you'll have practical skills you can actually use. Not ideas that sound nice but fall apart when your mind won't stop racing. You'll learn how to stop spirals, catch patterns before they drag you down, and deal with frustration, fear, pressure, and self-doubt in ways that don't leave you stuck.

Life throws plenty at you: exams, drama with friends, problems at home, and the constant pressure to figure everything out. This book shows you how to steady yourself and bounce back without pretending you need to be perfect.

It also tackles relationships, because other people can be confusing. You'll find ways to set boundaries, handle tension, and stop overthinking what someone meant in a text.

At its core, this is about you, not in a cheesy motivational way, but in a practical one. It's about understanding how your mind works and taking more control over how you respond. You don't need to change who you are. You learn how to handle things when your thoughts get noisy, stuck, or overwhelming.

This isn't a magic fix. It's a starting point for growth that actually makes sense and helps you feel stronger in the everyday moments that used to trip you up.

Ready to Try This Out?

If you've made it this far, that already says something. Maybe you're curious. Maybe you're tired of feeling stuck. Or maybe you're just hoping something in these pages makes a bit of a difference. Whatever brought you here, the next step is yours.

This book isn't something you have to race through or get right on the first try. It's meant to be used. Scribbled in. Dog-eared. Returned to on days when everything feels too loud or on days when things are quiet, and you just want to understand yourself better.

The tools inside aren't complicated, but they do ask you to show up. That means trying out exercises, even the ones that feel a little weird at first. It means pausing to think about your thoughts instead of brushing them off. It means noticing patterns, testing new ways to respond, and building new habits that make hard days a little easier to carry.

You don't have to rush. There's no deadline for figuring yourself out. The goal isn't to become someone else, it's to understand and support who you already are. That version of you deserves care, patience, and tools that actually help.

So, try the exercises. Ask yourself honest questions. Reflect. Repeat. Let this book be a space where you figure things out at your own pace, with no pressure to get it all right. You're allowed to grow on your own terms.

Start small—read a page, try one thing, and see the change.

📖How to Get the Most Out of This Book: 5-Step Learning Path for Parents & Teens

Based on feedback from thousands of parents, the most effective way to help teens grow through reading is to keep it consistent, stress-free and fun. To help your teen get the most out of this book, here's the simple learning path that parents say works best:

Step 1: Read in Small Bites

Parents recommend reading 1–2 chapters per week. This pace keeps things manageable and prevents overwhelm for busy teens.

Step 2: Share Back Weekly

Encourage your teen to retell what they learned, either orally or in writing. This boosts confidence, strengthens communication skills, and helps you naturally see their progress.

Step 3: Read Together, Not Alone

Many parents find that reading side-by-side or aloud together creates bonding moments. Teens open up more when parents show genuine interest in the same material.

Step 4: Make It Fun & Rewarding

Small incentives go a long way. Parents say that weekly rewards (like a favorite snack or extra screen time) and bigger milestone rewards (like a gift card or outing) keep teens motivated and looking forward to reading.

Step 5: Celebrate, Don't Criticize

If a chapter feels "boring" or "difficult," break it down into short talks, connect the ideas to real life, and celebrate small wins. Teens don't need to ace every single chapter; just applying even one lesson makes a difference.

🌟 Encouragement

Remember, the goal isn't perfection. Just showing up consistently with your teen makes a lasting impact.

If your teen learns even one meaningful lesson from this book, that's a job well done! 👏

CHAPTER 1:

Meet Your Mind and CBT - What's Going On Up There?

"The greatest weapon against stress is our ability to choose one thought over another."—

William James

HEY THERE. BEFORE we jump into anything deep, let's start with something simple: have you ever wondered why your mind feels like it has a mind of its own? One minute, you're fine, and the next, your thoughts are spiraling over something tiny, like a missed text or a weird look from someone in class. You're not alone. That rollercoaster going on in your head? It's not broken. It's actually working the way it's supposed to. But here's the good news: just because your brain has patterns doesn't mean you're stuck with them forever. In this chapter, we're going to get to know that busy brain of yours, how CBT (Cognitive Behavioral Therapy) helps it work better, and why understanding your thoughts is the first step to feeling more in control, even on the messiest days.

Your Brain Is Not Broken

Imagine your brain like a super-smart personal assistant who's always trying to keep you safe, even when it messes up a bit. That racing heart when you forget your homework? That's not a weakness. It's your brain reacting to what it thinks is a threat. It learned that pattern from somewhere, maybe from school pressure, past experiences, or just the way it's wired.

CBT helps you understand that these reactions aren't failures. They're messages. And while the messages can get scrambled, it doesn't mean the whole system is broken. In fact, your brain is doing exactly what it was built to do: notice danger, react fast, and push you to act. The problem is, sometimes it mistakes a teacher's raised eyebrow for a tiger attack. CBT gives you the tools to decode those messages and decide which ones deserve your attention.

In a study, brain imaging showed that people with anxiety and depression had heightened activity in the amygdala, the part of the brain that signals danger, even when the threat wasn't real. CBT helps calm this reaction by changing how the brain responds to stressful thoughts through targeted skills and reframing techniques.

How Thoughts Affect Feelings and Behaviors

Think of your thoughts like a pair of tinted glasses. If they're dark and cloudy, the world looks scary. If they're clear, everything feels more manageable. CBT is built on the idea that your thoughts shape how you feel, and that feeling shapes how you act. It's all connected. Let's break it down:

- You think: "Everyone's judging me at lunch."
- You feel: Nervous, embarrassed.
- You act: You avoid the cafeteria.

But what if that thought isn't completely true? What if most people are thinking about their own stuff? CBT teaches you to step back and examine the thought, like a detective asking, "Is this true? Is there another way to look at this?"

This connection between thoughts, emotions, and behavior is well-documented in research. Beck's Cognitive Model (Beck, 1967) laid the foundation for CBT by showing how negative automatic thoughts contribute to emotional struggles. By shifting those thoughts, behavior, and mood also improve.

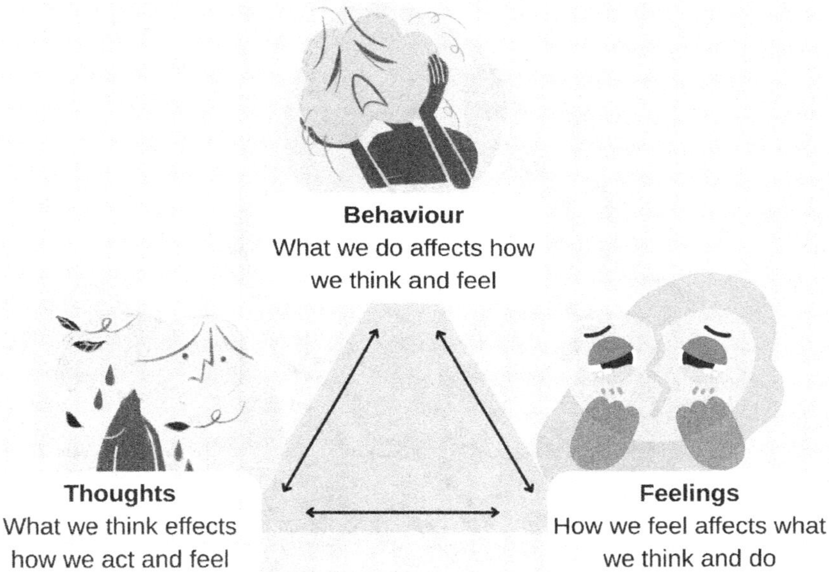

😱 When Your Brain Goes into "Alarm Mode"

Ever feel like your brain hits a panic button over something small, like getting left on read or forgetting a locker combination? That's your brain's alarm system, also known as the fight-flight-freeze response, kicking in.

Here's what happens: The amygdala (your brain's threat sensor) sends out a big "uh-oh" signal. Your body gets ready to either fight, run, or shut down. That's great if there's an actual emergency. But in everyday life, this alarm can go off too often and too loudly.

CBT gives you tools to calm that alarm. Breathing techniques, thought-challenging exercises, and exposure exercises help you train your brain to tell the difference between an actual threat and something that just feels scary. Over time, your alarm system gets smarter.

Research confirms that CBT is effective in reducing amygdala activity in people with anxiety disorders, showing measurable changes in how the brain reacts to perceived threats.

What Makes Your Brain Uniquely You

No two brains are the same. Yours has its own wiring, memories, strengths, and habits. Maybe you're a deep thinker. Maybe your brain jumps ahead to worst-case scenarios. Maybe you replay conversations and wonder what you should've said. All of that is part of what makes your brain yours.

CBT doesn't try to make everyone think the same way. It helps you get to know your own thought patterns and create healthier ways to respond to them. It's about working with your brain, not against it. Once you start to understand how your thoughts, feelings, and reactions connect, you can start to change the ones that don't help you.

This idea is supported by research on neuroplasticity. Studies show that CBT can literally change the structure and function of the brain through practice and repetition. That means the way you think and respond isn't fixed. It can grow, adapt, and improve.

📖 What is Cognitive Behavioral Therapy?

Cognitive Behavioral Therapy, or CBT for short, is like giving your brain a user manual. It's a science-backed method that helps people understand how their thoughts, feelings, and actions are connected and how to make those connections work better. Think of it like fixing a glitchy app. You don't throw out the whole phone; you just troubleshoot what's causing the problem.

🧠 Did You Know?

CBT (Cognitive Behavioral Therapy) works by helping you spot patterns in your thinking, just like a detective. It's one of the most effective tools used by therapists to treat anxiety and depression, even in kids and teens!

CBT is based on the idea that many of our struggles come from unhelpful thought patterns. When you change the way you think about something, you can change how you feel and what you do. It's been studied for decades, and studies show that CBT is highly effective in treating anxiety, depression, and stress-related issues.

🧑‍🎓 Why Is CBT Good for Teens?

Let's be real, being a teen can feel like you're juggling school, friends, family, hormones, and social media all at once. It's easy to feel overwhelmed or unsure about how to deal with pressure, disappointment, or anxiety. That's where CBT comes in. It's not some mysterious therapy made for adults. It's actually designed to work for real-life stuff, like overthinking after a text conversation, panicking about grades, or feeling low when friendships change.

A study found that CBT helped teens reduce symptoms of anxiety and depression in both school and clinical settings. It works because it gives you skills, not just advice. You learn how to spot unhelpful thoughts and replace them with more helpful ones. You get to practice this with the support of a therapist, a counselor, or even through guided self-help programs.

Why We Feel Stuff? 😮💬💕

Emotions aren't random drama—they're signals. Anger shows a boundary was crossed, sadness signals loss, and joy marks what feels right. CBT teaches us to read these cues: anxiety means you care, guilt points to values, and loneliness reminds you to connect. Feelings aren't problems; they're messages that something matters.

Moods are background noise, while big emotions demand attention. A snack or rest can fix a mood, but bigger feelings need to be named and worked through. Avoiding them only makes them louder. Real strength comes from facing emotions, not hiding them.

Emotions are part of being human, not flaws to fix. Learning to listen to them helps you grow instead of getting stuck.

Typical Structure of CBT Sessions

If you've never had therapy before, CBT might sound like a big step. But it's not as formal or intimidating as it sounds. A typical CBT session is more like a team meeting between you and your therapist. You're not just sitting and talking about your feelings randomly. You're learning how to track your thoughts, figure out which ones are helpful or unhelpful, and test new ways of thinking.

Here's what a session might look like:

- You start by checking in about your week and anything that came up.
- You might review your thought records (basically notes about stuff that triggered big feelings).
- You and your therapist look at a specific situation where you felt upset, anxious, or stuck.
- You break down what thoughts you had and how you reacted.
- Then you explore other ways to think about that same situation and plan ways to try out new strategies before your next session.

It's more practical than you might think. You won't be lying on a couch while someone asks about your childhood every week. It's action-based and goal-focused.

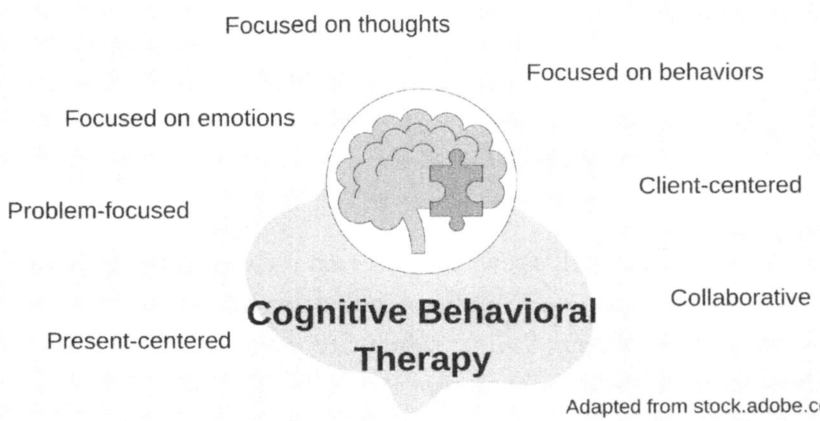

Adapted from stock.adobe.com

CBT Techniques Used in Therapy

The following techniques are used in therapy:

i. Cognitive Restructuring

This is a fancy name for something super helpful. It just means learning how to catch those automatic negative thoughts that pop up and seeing if they really make sense. It's kind of like arguing with a mean comment in your head and standing up for yourself.

Let's say you bomb a math quiz and think, "I'm so dumb." CBT helps you press pause and ask, "Wait, is that 100% true? Or am I just feeling discouraged?" You learn to spot exaggerations, filter out false beliefs, and reframe your thinking to something more accurate, like, "I didn't do great on this quiz, but I can study differently next time."

It's the mental version of checking the mirror when you think your hair looks awful, only to realize it's not that bad after all.

ii. Exposure Therapy Techniques

If something scares you, like speaking in front of a group or going to school after a panic attack, your instinct might be to avoid it. But avoidance makes anxiety grow louder over time. CBT helps you face those fears gradually, step by step, until they're not so scary anymore.

This process is called exposure. It's not about throwing you into terrifying situations. It's about making a ladder and climbing it one step at a time. For example:

- Step 1: Imagine giving a speech.
- Step 2: Practice in front of your mirror.
- Step 3: Record yourself on your phone.
- Step 4: Share with a friend.
- Step 5: Present in class.

That's how CBT helps rewire your brain to stop treating that fear as danger. Over time, you gain confidence and control.

Remember in *Doctor Strange* when Stephen is terrified of his new reality? He doesn't suddenly master magic. He fails, gets frustrated, but keeps showing up. That's exposure in action, learning through repetition and support.

Cognitive Behavioral Therapy Tools

Cognitive Restructuring
Exploring causes of faulty thinking and negative thoughts and then reframing and restructuring them.

Interoceptive Exposure
Purposeful exposure to sensations of panic to make you understand that those sensations aren't dangerous.

Exposure and Response Prevention
Purposefully exposing self to triggers and mindfully controlling the response.

Signs You Might Need CBT

You don't need to be at your lowest point to benefit from CBT. In fact, many teens find it useful even before things get too overwhelming. Here are some signs it might help:

- You often feel stuck in negative thoughts that are hard to shake.
- You avoid things because of anxiety or fear.
- You feel like your emotions are running the show.
- You have a hard time bouncing back from tough situations.
- You want tools to understand yourself better and manage stress.

CBT doesn't make life perfect, but it gives you a mental toolbox. And when life throws something at you, you don't just stand there; you reach for a tool.

The Thought-Feeling-Action Loop

Imagine this: You see a message from your friend, and they've left you on read. Instantly, a thought pops up: *"They must be mad at me."* That thought doesn't just sit there. It kicks off a chain reaction. You start to feel anxious, maybe even a little hurt. Then you act; you ignore them, too, or you start overthinking the last thing you said.

This is what CBT calls the Thought-Feeling-Action loop. It's one of the most important ideas in CBT. Why? Because it shows how your brain is constantly creating patterns, and the good news is, you can learn to change them.

A thought leads to a feeling. That feeling influences what you do. And your action can feed back into how you think again. It's a loop that runs all day. But once you start noticing it, you get the power to step in and shift it.

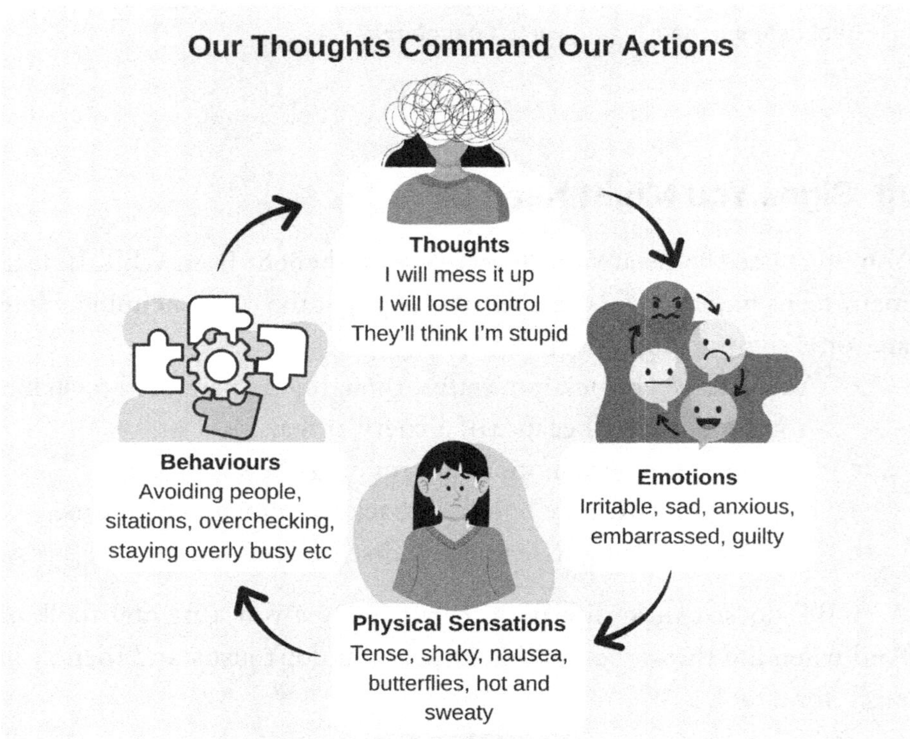

Real Teen Examples of the Loop in Action

You might be wondering, "What does this look like in real life?" Let's break it down with some real teen moments.

Example 1: Social Anxiety

Thought: *"If I speak in class, I'll say something dumb."*

Feeling: Nervous, embarrassed, tense

Action: You stay silent, even when you know the answer

Result: You feel frustrated and left out, and the thought gets stronger

Now let's reframe that using CBT skills:

New Thought: *"Even if I stumble, at least I'm trying, and I might do better next time."*

New Feeling: Slight nerves, but also courage

New Action: You give it a shot and speak up

New Result: You might feel proud or more confident, and the original thought starts to weaken

Example 2: Self-Esteem

Thought: "They didn't invite me. I must be boring."

Feeling: Sad, unwanted

Action: You isolate yourself and scroll through social media

Result: You feel even more left out

Now with a CBT check-in:

New Thought: "Maybe it was a small hangout. That doesn't mean they don't like me."

New Feeling: Disappointed, but not crushed

New Action: You text another friend to hang out

New Result: You stay connected and challenge the original belief

These examples show that a small shift in thinking can create a totally different emotional and behavioral outcome.

Okay, so now you've seen how the loop works. But here's the best part: it doesn't take a considerable change to turn things around.

☆ How Changing One Part Changes Everything

The best part about understanding this loop is realizing that you don't need to fix everything at once. You can step in at *any* part of the loop. That's the key CBT insight. Change your thought, and your feelings shift. Change your action, and your thoughts might follow.

For instance, let's say you're feeling unmotivated, and the thought is, *"I'll probably mess this up, so why try?"* You don't have to wait to feel better before doing something. CBT encourages you to take action, even a small one, because action can help reshape thought.

This is often called *behavioral activation*. It's especially useful when emotions are too heavy to think clearly. Instead of trying to think your way out of it, you do something positive and let your brain catch up.

Want to try this out for yourself? Here's a simple way to see how your own Thought-Feeling-Action loop works.

Drawing Your Own Loop

One way to really understand this is to draw your own Thought-Feeling-Action loop. Here's how:

1. Think of a recent situation that got to you emotionally.
2. Write down the thought you had.
3. Describe the feeling that came next.
4. List the action you took (or avoided).
5. Ask yourself: Did the action make things better, worse, or the same?

Now try changing just the thought. What could a more balanced thought look like? Imagine what that new loop would look like with a different feeling and a different response.

This exercise helps you see that you're not stuck in any loop forever. With practice, you can shape it into something that works *for you*, not against you.

How to Spot Judgmental Brain Messages

Have you ever noticed how your brain can act like a critic? Let's understand it with a story.

Jada sat at the back of the classroom, replaying the moment she stumbled on her words during her presentation. "That was so awkward," she muttered under her breath. As her classmates moved on, her brain wasn't done yet. "Why can't you be more like Maya? She nailed it."

Her stomach twisted. She didn't raise her hand for the rest of the class. Later that day, her friend Kai noticed she was quiet. "You okay?" Jada shrugged. "I bombed that presentation. I sounded like a total mess." Kai blinked. "Really? I thought you were brave for going first."

Sometimes, your brain acts like a harsh critic, but that doesn't mean it's telling the truth. These are called judgmental thoughts, and they often show up when we're feeling unsure or stressed. CBT helps you recognize these thoughts so they don't run the show.

A good trick is to ask: *"Would I say this to a friend?"* If the answer is no, that thought might not be worth keeping around.

Judgmental thoughts are quick to jump in, but that doesn't mean they should get the final word. Spotting them is the first step toward turning down their volume.

So what do you do with those judgmental thoughts? One powerful trick is learning to notice them without doing what they say.

You need to learn how to select your thoughts just the same way you select your clothes everyday. this is a power you can cultivate.
Elizabeth Gilbert

🧐 Learning to Observe, Not Obey, Your Thoughts

Just because a thought pops into your head doesn't mean you have to follow it. This is where thought defusion comes in, a CBT strategy that helps you create space between you and your thoughts.

Take the example of Amir. When Amir forgot his lines during theater practice, his brain jumped in fast. "You're going to mess up again tomorrow," it warned. He almost believed it, until he remembered what his counselor taught him. Instead of thinking, I'm going to fail again, Amir whispered, "I'm having the thought that *I'm going to fail again.*"

It felt weird. But saying it that way made the thought seem smaller, like it was floating just outside his head instead of living inside him. That night, he practiced his lines again, but this time with a little more confidence. That small shift put the thought outside of him instead of inside his identity.

It's like seeing a cloud pass across the sky. You can notice it without jumping into it. You don't have to wrestle with every thought that comes by. Sometimes, the best move is to let it drift and keep going. It's just how, in *Spider-Man: Into the Spider-Verse*, Miles hears so many voices telling him he's not ready. But the real change happens when he decides to trust his actions, not the doubt in his head. That's what CBT encourages: stepping back, seeing the thought, and deciding what *you* want to do next.

Another fun way to take the power away from those tricky thoughts is to give them silly names. Yes, really.

🎭 Giving Your Thoughts Silly Names

Sometimes, when thoughts feel heavy or overwhelming, adding a bit of humor can change the whole mood. Instead of getting stuck in the same old "what-if" spiral, try naming that thought something ridiculous.

That voice that says, "*You'll mess it up*"? Call it "Doubtzilla." The one that whispers, "*Nobody likes you*"? Maybe that's "Drama Duck."

The perfectionist voice? Try "Captain Impossible."

Naming your thoughts helps you remember they're not facts. They're just old patterns your brain repeats. And once you name them, you can laugh a little and say, *"Thanks, Drama Duck, but I've got this."*

This method comes from Acceptance and Commitment Therapy (a close cousin of CBT), and research supports it. It was found in a study that giving distance from thoughts reduced their emotional impact. Humor and creativity are tools you can use right alongside logic.

📌 Chapter Wrap-Up

By now, you've seen just how much your thoughts, feelings, and actions are connected and how your brain plays a big part in all of it. CBT doesn't promise to make life perfect, but it *does* give you tools to understand what's happening inside you and what you can do about it.

Your thoughts don't have to be bullies. Your emotions aren't enemies. And your brain isn't broken. It's learning. Changing. Growing. Just like you.

Every time you pause, question a thought, or try a new habit, you're reshaping your path. Not all at once. But in real, meaningful ways. The point isn't to be perfect, it's to be curious, kind to yourself, and open to growth.

Now that you've met your mind and gotten a peek at what's going on upstairs, it's time to catch those tricky thoughts before they catch you. Get ready to dive into Chapter 2!

🏠 Parents' Corner: Thought Swap Game

Sit down with your teen and each write down one unhelpful thought you've had recently (you can keep it light or silly).

Then, switch papers and try to help each other come up with a more helpful version of that thought. For Example:

Teen's thought: ***"I always mess up."***

Parents' reframe: ***"Messing up sometimes just means you're learning."***

This helps both of you practice spotting and reshaping tricky thoughts together.

🔑 Key Takeaways

- Your brain reacts to emotions, but you can learn how to respond calmly.
- Not all brain "facts" are true, like the left/right brain myth.
- Teen brains are still growing, which means they're super adaptable.
- Good habits and decision-making come from practice, not perfection.
- Understanding how your brain works helps you make better choices.

🕵️ Exercise 1: Thought Detective

Every thought tells a story — some are helpful, some need a rewrite. Write down one thought that popped into your head today. Then, investigate it like a detective looking for clues.

Step 1: Write the thought:

____

____

____

Step 2: Gather the evidence.

____

____

____

____

✅ Facts that support this thought:

____

____

____

____

❌ Facts that go against this thought:

____

____

____

Step 3: Final verdict — helpful or unhelpful?

____

____

____

____

📕 Exercise 2: Feelings Journal

Emotions change throughout the day. Tracking them helps you notice patterns. Try this for one week — write about your feelings three times a day.

Time of Day 🌞⛅🌙	What were you doing?	What were you thinking?	How did you feel (1–2 words)?
Morning ☀	____________ ____________	____________ ____________	____________ ____________
Afternoon ⛅	____________ ____________	____________ ____________	____________ ____________
Evening 🌙	____________ ____________	____________ ____________	____________ ____________

⭐ After one week, look for clues: When do you feel your best? What tends to make your mood dip or rise?

CHAPTER 2:

Catching Thoughts - Not Every Thought Is True

"Don't believe everything you think. Thoughts are just that—thoughts."

— Allan Lokos

HAVE YOU EVER had a thought that instantly made your heart race or your stomach twist, even if nothing was really wrong? That's your brain reacting, but not always with the truth. This chapter is all about learning to question those thoughts instead of automatically believing them. You'll step into "thought detective" mode, explore mind traps like catastrophizing and personalization, and get the hang of rewriting harsh self-talk into something more balanced and helpful.

You'll also try tools that help calm overthinking, like drawing out your "What if?" spirals or flipping the script when your brain turns mean. The goal? To help you spot when your thoughts are working against you and show you how to take back control, one small shift at a time.

🤯 Mind Traps

Sometimes your brain feels like a helpful teammate, offering support and ideas. But other times, it throws you into mental booby traps without warning. These are called cognitive distortions, thought habits that seem believable but are actually twisted and exaggerated. Everyone falls into these traps sometimes, especially during stress, conflict, or uncertainty.

Think of them like glitches in your thinking software. CBT teaches you how to catch these bugs and update the program. Once you know what these mental traps look like, you can stop them from running your thoughts in circles.

🤖 What Are Cognitive Distortions?

Cognitive distortions are sneaky thinking errors that twist reality. They're automatic, which means they pop up fast and feel true, but they aren't facts. They can make you feel anxious, sad, angry, or stuck, even when the situation doesn't really call for it.

Here's a quick analogy: Imagine you're wearing a pair of cracked sunglasses. Everything you see is a little off, but you don't notice because you've had them on for so long. CBT helps you take those off, clean the lens, and see what's actually happening.

Psychologist Aaron T. Beck first outlined many of these distorted thinking patterns when developing CBT. Research shows that helping teens identify and name these patterns can lead to significant improvement in mood and decision-making.

Cognitive Distortions

Cognitive distortions are inacurate or faulty ways of thinking that you often believe to be true.

They are also known as:

Thinking Errors

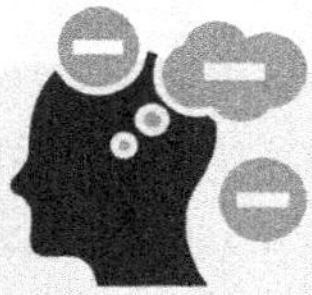

Negative Thinking Patterns

Automatic Negative Thoughts (ANTs)

Unhelpful Thinking Styles

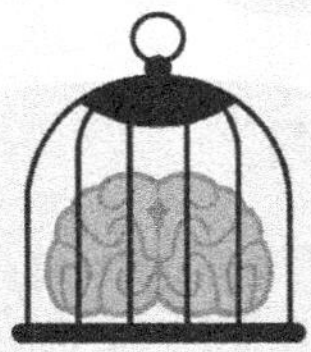

Thinking Traps

Heading	Key Idea	Example / Action
Thought Detective Mode	Not every thought is true; pause and check if it helps or hurts.	Ask: "Is this a fact or an assumption?"
Helpful vs Unhelpful Thoughts	Helpful = realistic and calming. Unhelpful = extreme, negative, or unfair.	Helpful: "I can prepare." Unhelpful: "I'll never pass."
Clues a Thought Is Lying	Uses extremes, mind-reading, or no evidence.	"K" text → assume anger. Instead, consider other reasons.
Thought Journals	Write situation, thought, feeling, and action to spot patterns.	Repeating "I'm not good enough" → challenge with a fairer view.

🚨 Example: All-or-Nothing Thinking

Ever failed one quiz and thought, "Well, that's it; I'm a total failure"? That's all-or-nothing thinking, also called black-and-white thinking. It's when your brain turns a situation into either 100% success or total disaster, with no middle ground.

Let's go Marvel for a second: imagine if Peter Parker gave up being Spider-Man just because he messed up once. "I couldn't stop the robbery. Guess I'm the worst superhero ever." Sounds dramatic, right? That's what this trap does; it pushes you into extremes.

In real life, most things fall in between. You might mess up one test but still do great overall. You might have a bad day, but that doesn't mean every day will be like that.

🌪️ Example: Catastrophizing

Now picture this: your best friend doesn't text back for hours. Your brain says, "They must hate me. I probably did something wrong. Maybe they never want to talk again." That's catastrophizing, imagining the worst-case scenario, even without any proof.

This mind trap takes a small bump and turns it into a disaster movie. It's like dropping a glass of water and assuming the whole house will flood. Studies on adolescents show that catastrophizing is a common habit in anxious thinking, but CBT helps reduce it by teaching how to slow down and question that inner narrator.

🎯 Example: Personalization

Here's another one: you walk into class, and the teacher seems a little cold. Your brain instantly whispers, "It's my fault. I must have done something wrong." That's personalization, when your mind blames you for things that probably have nothing to do with you.

Truth is, maybe your teacher just had a rough morning. But personalization makes it all about you, even when it's not. Over time, this trap chips away at your confidence and makes you feel responsible for things outside your control.

🎨 Comic Strip Activity to Spot Mind Traps

Try this: draw a short three-panel comic strip showing a character facing a situation, reacting with a distorted thought, and then "rewriting" it with a healthier one.

Panel 1: Mia sees her two friends whispering in the hallway.

Panel 2: Thought bubble: "They're talking about me. I knew they didn't really like me."

Panel 3: Reframe bubble: "Wait, maybe they're just planning a surprise. Or talking about something totally different."

This activity helps your brain start to recognize how fast these traps appear and how you can rewrite the script with more balanced thinking.

🧩 How to Name and Defuse Mind Traps

You can't fix a bug you don't notice. That's why the first step is to name the trap. Is it all or nothing? Catastrophizing? Personalizing? Once you name it, it loses a bit of its power. Next, try these tools:

- **Reality Check:** What's the evidence for this thought?
- **Flip the Thought:** What's another way to see this?
- **Name It Out Loud:** "Oh, I'm catastrophizing right now."

The goal isn't to be thought-free. It's to get better at spotting the tricks your brain plays and calling them out before they drag you down.

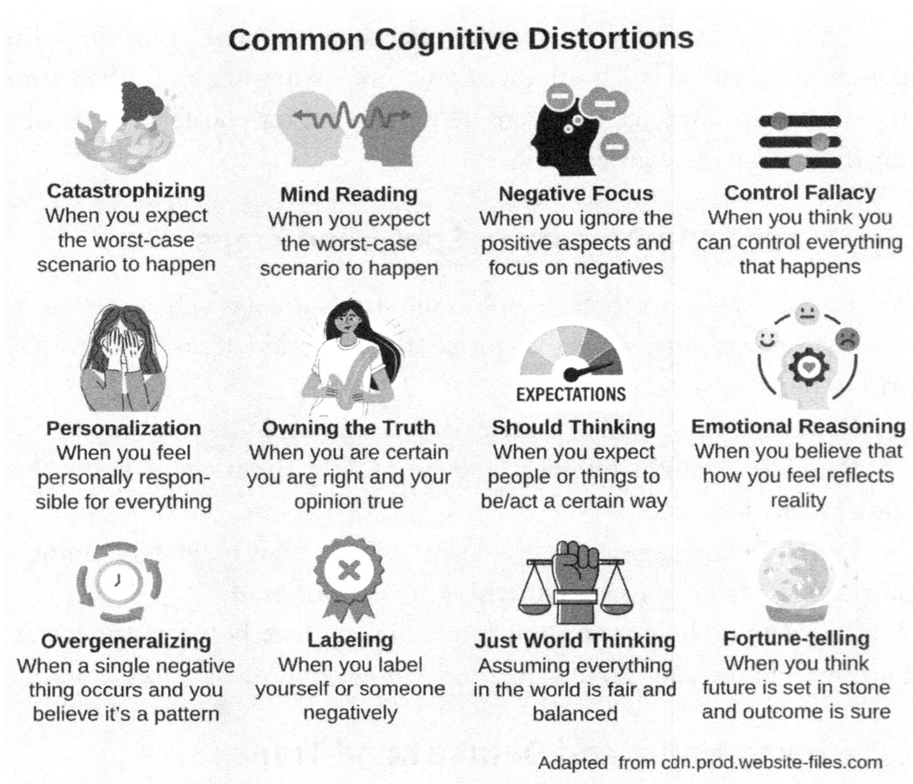

"What If?" Spiral

Have you ever sat down to relax, and then suddenly your brain starts spinning with "What if…" questions?

"What if I fail the test?"

"What if my friend stops liking me?"

"What if I embarrass myself tomorrow?"

It starts with one thought, then picks up speed until you're stuck in a tornado of worries. This is the "What If?" spiral. It begins quietly but builds fast, often turning a tiny concern into a full-blown crisis, at least in your head. The spiral is your brain's way of trying to prepare for danger, but it ends up creating more stress instead of solving anything.

Let's break it down and figure out how to stop the spiral before it drags you under.

😟 How Overthinking Starts and Grows

Imagine this: you send a message to your group chat, and no one replies for hours. That tiny silence turns into "What if they're annoyed at me?" Then comes "What if I said something wrong?" followed by "What if I don't get invited next time?" and finally, "What if I lose all my friends?"

It's like standing at the top of a slide and suddenly slipping, except this slide goes down through layer after layer of worry. The first thought might seem small, but it unlocks a chain reaction.

Research from the University of Amsterdam shows that overthinking is linked with increased anxiety, sleep problems, and trouble making decisions in teens. The more time you spend imagining disasters, the more powerless and anxious you feel in real life, even when nothing bad is actually happening.

You're creating problems in your head again! STOP THAT

🛡️ What Your "What Ifs" Are Trying to Protect You From

Your brain doesn't spiral for no reason. These questions come from a place of fear and a desire to protect yourself. When your brain says, "What if I fail?" it's trying to prepare for failure so you don't get caught off guard; it's trying to keep you safe.

Think of it like a guard dog that barks at every single sound, even harmless ones. Its heart is in the right place, but it ends up keeping you up all night for nothing.

CBT teaches that instead of letting the "guard dog" run wild, you can train it to pause and check if there's actually a threat. Once you understand the purpose of worry (protection), it becomes easier to thank it but not obey it.

👁 Visualizing Your Worry Spiral and Stopping It Early

One useful tool is to draw your worry spiral. Grab a pen and sketch a swirl. In the center, write your first "What if?" (e.g., "What if I mess up my presentation?"). Then, in the outer rings, write what that thought snowballs into: "People will laugh," "I'll never be taken seriously," "My teacher will think I'm lazy."

Now pause. Ask yourself: which of these has actually happened? Which is just imagination?

Here's another way to picture it. In The *Maze Runner*, Thomas wakes up in a terrifying, unknown place. He has no memory, just questions. If he gave in to panic, he'd never find the path out. But by staying calm and observing his surroundings, he figures out the maze, one step at a time. That's what you're doing here, calming the panic so you can actually think.

A study found that teens who used visual techniques like spiral diagrams or mind maps to externalize their worries experienced lower stress and improved problem-solving skills.

📝 Writing a "What Else Could Happen?" List

This is a power move: take your original "What if?" question and create a list of other possible outcomes, some neutral, some positive.

Let's say your worry is: *"What if I freeze during my class speech?"* Now write five other things that could happen:

I might be nervous at first, but then I'll settle in.

1. People might not even notice if I pause.
2. My friends will probably cheer me on.
3. I could actually do better than I expect.
4. Even if I mess up, it's not the end of the world; I'll learn from it.

This activity doesn't try to erase your fear. It just reminds your brain that fear isn't the only option. There are more doors than the one your anxiety wants you to walk through.

Overthinking might feel like it gives you control, but really, it steals your peace. The "What If?" spiral is one of the most common tricks anxiety plays, and now you know how to spot it. When it shows up, pause. Ask yourself if the thought is helpful. Imagine your spiral, or make your "What else could happen?" list.

You don't have to silence your thoughts; you just need to stop letting them drag you around.

Thoughts Are Not Facts

Putting some distance between your reactions and yourself can change your relationship to your thoughts.

Stuck on a negative thought? Ask yourself:

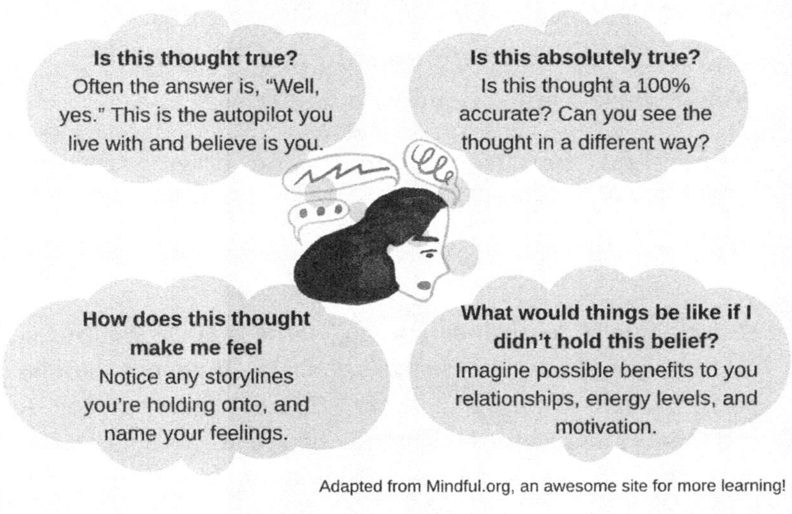

Adapted from Mindful.org, an awesome site for more learning!

Challenge Accepted

Sometimes your brain acts like it's always right. It throws out thoughts like, "I'll never be good at anything," or "Everyone hates me," and expects you to just accept them. But what if those thoughts were more like rumors than facts?

In CBT, one powerful strategy is to *challenge* those automatic thoughts instead of just believing them. It's not about arguing with your brain all day. It's about asking smart questions, the kind lawyers ask in court to find out if your brain is being fair or just dramatic. Let's break it down.

Socratic Questions: Become a Thought Detective

You might've heard of Socrates. He was a Greek philosopher who loved asking questions, especially the kind that made people think deeper. In CBT, we borrow that idea.

Imagine your thought is: *"I'm never going to make real friends."* Now hit it with questions like:

- Is this 100% true?
- What's the actual evidence for and against this?
- Have I felt this way before and turned out okay?
- What would I tell a friend who said this?

These questions force your brain to slow down and look at the thought like a science experiment, not a scary truth.

Fun Fact

Your brain talks to itself all day long, up to 60,000 thoughts a day, according to some cognitive scientists. But here's the wild part: studies estimate that about 80% of them are negative, and 95% are the same thoughts you had yesterday. Learning to challenge and change these can literally change the way your brain works.

In a study, it was found that teens who practiced Socratic questioning over four weeks showed reduced anxiety and improved mood compared to those who didn't. Their brains literally got better at fact-checking the drama.

Separate Yourself from Your Thoughts

Roleplay Thought Battles

Think of your thoughts like characters in a debate club. One side says, *"I'm a total failure."* The other side says, *"That's not fair, you just had a rough day."* Your job? Let both speak, then decide who's actually making sense.

Here's a scene:

Negative Thought (aka "The Judge"):

"You always mess things up. You didn't even get picked for the team."

Challenger (aka "The Lawyer"):

"That's not true. You did great in your last game, and the coach even said you improved."

The Verdict (aka "You"):

"Okay, maybe I didn't get picked this time. But I'm still getting better, and this doesn't define me."

It sounds cheesy at first, but it actually works. Try doing it in your journal or even voice recording it on your phone. Giving your thoughts names or voices can help you see how different they are and which ones deserve airtime.

In *Stranger Things*, remember how Will hears "The Mind Flayer" whispering dark stuff to him? That voice seemed real. But once his friends helped him challenge it, he realized it was the enemy talking. Your harsh thoughts are like that; they can sound convincing, but they're not always true.

Chapter Wrap-Up

Anxiety doesn't always show up as panic attacks or major meltdowns. Sometimes, it's quieter. A thought that sneaks in and makes your stomach turn. A moment where your brain won't stop playing the worst-case scenario. A voice in your head that sounds like truth but feels like fear.

This chapter was about naming those moments and learning what to do with them. You explored how anxiety works, why your brain sometimes treats normal stuff like danger, and how you can interrupt those mental spirals before they take over.

You learned how to:

- Spot your anxiety signs early
- Understand what triggers your anxious thoughts
- Flip negative self-talk into something more honest and kind
- Step back and ask: "Is this actually true?"
- Practice simple tools like the "What else could happen?" list, affirmation cards, and thought challenges

Anxiety doesn't get the last word. Not anymore. Whether it shows up as "What if?" spirals, harsh inner criticism, or worst-case daydreams, you now have ways to slow it down, question it, and choose better thoughts. This chapter gave you tools. Now it's about practice. Try one technique this week. Write out one flipped thought. Catch one "What if?" spiral before it grows. You don't have to do all of it. Just one thing is enough to remind yourself:

You are not your anxiety.

You are not your worst thought.

You're someone learning to think differently. And that counts.

As you've learned that not every thought is true—next up, we're exploring how big feelings aren't failures and how to handle them without freaking out.

🏠 Parents' Corner: Let's Think Together

Activity 1: "True or Just Loud?" Game

Sit down together and take turns reading these thoughts out loud. For each one, decide together: Is this thought 100% true, or just loud?

"Nobody likes me."

"If I fail once, it means I'm a failure."

"They didn't text back, so they must be mad."

"It's okay to make mistakes and try again."

"Everyone else has it figured out but me."

After each one, flip it! Rewrite the thought into something kinder and more accurate. You can use a whiteboard, sticky notes, or just shout it out like a game show.

Activity 2: Backyard Worry Spiral Picnic

This one is part fun, part reflection.

Make sandwiches or snacks together and head to your backyard, living room floor, or even a pillow fort. Talk about one recent *"What if?"* spiral you each had. Then, map it out together: what started it, where it went, and what might have helped calm it down.

Use the spiral drawing activity from earlier in the chapter to sketch it out while you munch. End the picnic by writing one kind sentence to yourself and reading it out loud to each other.

Key Takeaways

- Your thoughts are not always facts, just because a thought is loud doesn't mean it's true.
- Overthinking creates stress, but tools like visualizing worry spirals can help you stop the cycle early.
- Flipping negative thoughts into kinder, more accurate ones builds emotional strength, not fake positivity.
- Socratic questioning ("Is this 100% true?") can help you challenge and reframe self-critical beliefs.
- Practicing with real-life scenarios and affirmation cards strengthens your ability to think flexibly and respond wisely.

📱 Exercise 1: Social Scroll Check

Your feed affects how you feel — more than you might notice. Take 5–10 minutes to scroll through your favorite app.

Step 1: Mark Your Reactions

Highlight posts that make you feel good, inspired, or calm.

Highlight posts that make you feel jealous, sad, or stressed.

Step 2: Write Down Your Reflections

What kinds of posts made you feel good?

What kinds made you feel worse?

What can you do to create a happier, healthier feed?

💡 Try it again in a week and see if your "green zone" grows.

🤳 Exercise 2: Self-Love Selfie

You are your own best hype team. Take a selfie (or draw one) that captures who you are today — no filters needed. Next to it, write three things you genuinely appreciate about yourself:

🩶1. ______________________________

🩶2. ______________________________

🩶3. ______________________________

Optional: Add doodles, affirmations, or fun captions like you would for a post — but just for you.

Reflection: How did it feel to celebrate yourself without comparing?

CHAPTER 3:

Feelings Aren't Failures - How to Handle Big Emotions

"Feelings are much like waves, we can't stop them from coming, but we can choose which ones to surf."

— Jonatan Mårtensson

'BIG' EMOTIONS CAN be like surprise guests; noisy, messy, and they arrive when you least expect them. One minute you're chill, the next you're all teary-eyed or feeling like you're gonna explode. But the thing is: Those feelings aren't evidence of weakness. They're simply messages coming from your brain, and naming those emotions? That's one of the smartest moves you can make. It's not just something therapists say to sound fancy; it's backed by science.

✏️The Power of Naming Your Feelings

When you give a feeling a name, something cool happens in your brain. Studies using brain scans found that naming emotions reduces activity in the amygdala, the area that sets off your emotional alarms, and increases activity in the thinking part of your brain, the prefrontal cortex. That means you move from reacting to responding.

Let's say you're angry. Saying "I'm mad" out loud doesn't make it disappear, but it stops it from growing like a monster in the dark. Now you've spotted it. And that gives you control.

One teen I worked with, Maria, would say she felt "off" all the time. But when we broke it down, she discovered that sometimes she was sad, at other times frustrated, and sometimes overwhelmed. Her coping skills got sharper once she could spot the difference. She knew what she was actually dealing with and could act accordingly.

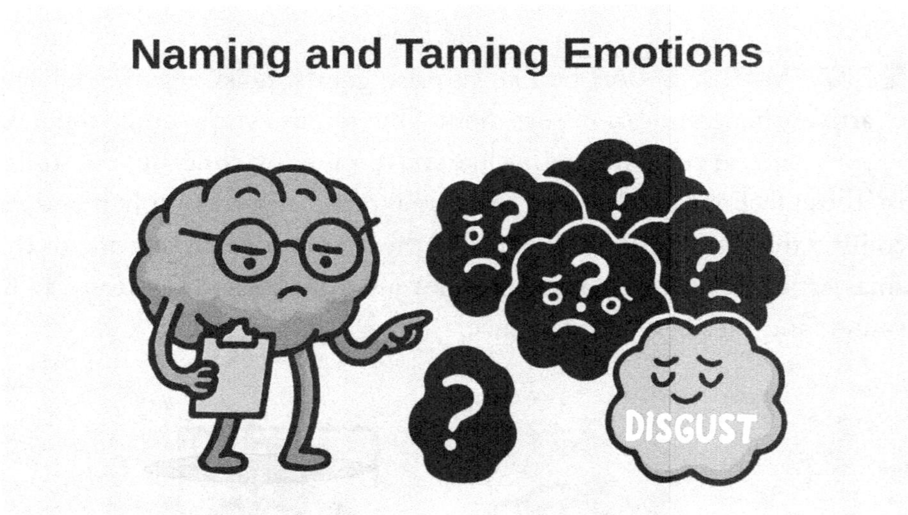

🎨 Emotion Wheel Activity

Here's a visual way to help: the Emotion Wheel. Think of it like a color wheel, but for feelings. You start with the big basic ones: happy, sad, angry, afraid, surprised, and disgusted. Then, like zooming in, you get more specific: is your "sad" more like "disappointed" or "lonely"? Is your "angry" more like "annoyed" or "furious"?

Try this: Print an emotion wheel or draw one with your own colors. For a few days, check in with it like a mood radar. "Where am I on the wheel right now?" It helps you to get better at reading your own emotional weather.

This action is, in particular, beneficial to children diagnosed with ADHD or who might struggle with identifying what each emotion entails. Visual tools create shortcuts to self-awareness.

😭 Why Avoiding Feelings Makes Them Louder

You might think avoiding emotions is smart, like ignoring a smoke alarm because you're too busy to deal with it. But just like smoke alarms, emotions don't stop screaming when ignored. They build pressure.

Let's use a pop culture example: In "Encanto," Luisa suppresses how overwhelmed she is until her strength begins to fade. Her song "Surface Pressure" is a musical version of literally stuffing down emotions. Spoiler: It doesn't go great for her until she opens up about what she's feeling.

Avoiding emotions might feel safer in the moment, but research shows it can heighten anxiety and even physical stress. When you stuff feelings down, they don't disappear; they just get shoved down and resurface in unexpected ways (snapping at someone, headaches, withdrawal).

CBT teaches that facing the emotion, even a little, helps shrink its power.

🧠Did You Know?

Researchers have found that just naming a feeling can lower activity in the emotional alarm center of your brain, "the amygdala,"and increase calm thinking from the prefrontal cortex. So saying "I'm feeling overwhelmed" is actually a brain hack, not a weakness!

🤗 How Naming Calms the Brain

Let's get nerdy for a second. Neuroscientists at UCLA discovered that when people labeled their emotions, their brains lit up in new ways. The part responsible for emotional reactivity quieted down, and the part that helps us reason and plan kicked in.

This is why CBT emphasizes emotional labeling as an early intervention tool. It's like putting a leash on a wild animal; not to hurt it, but to keep it from running wild and dragging you through the dirt.

Try this CBT trick: instead of saying "I'm so overwhelmed," say "I'm having the feeling of overwhelm." It creates a little space between you and the emotion. You're still feeling it, but it's not swallowing you whole.

🌡️ Mood Meter

Once you get good at naming your emotions, the next step is learning to track them. That's where the Mood Meter comes in. It's an easy, colorful way to check in with yourself each day. Think of it as a thermometer for your emotions, an aid to figuring out what's heating up and what's cooling down inside you.

📅 Daily Mood Check-Ins

A mood check-in is just a quick moment where you stop and ask, "How am I feeling right now?" You can do it in the morning, before bed, or even after school. No big speech, no journaling essay, just a word or two to describe where you're at.

Some teens use a calendar and draw a little emoji each day: 😄, 😐, 😢, 😤. Others use apps that track mood with simple sliders. What matters most is making it a habit. Once a day is enough to start noticing patterns.

🚦 Color-Coded Mood Charts

Here's a fun way to visualize what's going on inside: grab four colors and make your own mood chart.

🔴Red = high energy, unpleasant (angry, overwhelmed)
🟡Yellow = high energy, pleasant (excited, playful)
🔵Blue = low energy, unpleasant (sad, tired)
🟢Green = low energy, pleasant (calm, relaxed)

Ask yourself each day: What color am I in? Plot your moods through the week. It's not about staying in the "green" box all the time. It's about understanding why you shift and what helps you move between zones.

This is especially useful for kids who are neurodivergent or struggle with emotional regulation; it makes moods something you can see and work with

🔗 Connecting Moods to Triggers

Now that you're tracking moods, you can start linking them to what's happening around you. Did you always feel blue after scrolling through certain accounts? Did yellow pop up after hanging out with a specific friend?

CBT calls this trigger awareness. It means you're learning what events, people, or thoughts lead to certain moods. And that gives you a choice. You can avoid certain triggers, plan how to handle them, or simply understand yourself better.

Example: Maya noticed she always hit the "red zone" after school on Tuesdays. Turns out, she had P.E. followed by math, her two hardest classes. Just knowing this helped her tell her mom she needed quiet time after school instead of jumping straight into chores.

📝Mood Journaling Prompts

Want to go a little deeper? Try these short journaling prompts to explore your feelings:

- "Today I felt ________ because ________."
- "Something that made me feel better was ________."
- "One thing that surprised me about my mood today was ________."

Keep your answers short and real—no need for big paragraphs; just truth in your own words.

Remember that big emotions aren't enemies; they're signals. Here's what anger, sadness, and anxiety are trying to tell you, and tools to handle them.

Emotion	What It's Trying to Tell You	Helpful Tools (CBT-based)
Anger	Acts like a bodyguard when you feel hurt, disrespected, or ignored.	Use an "anger thermometer" (rate 1–10), clench and release fists, pause with phrases like "Let me think before I speak."
Sadness	Signals loss or need for comfort; it slows you down to process.	Make a comfort kit (snacks, playlist, journal), reach out to someone you trust, change scenery with a walk or new space.
Anxiety	Works like a warning bell or scout, even for imagined danger.	Slow deep breathing, thought-challenging ("worst, best, most likely outcome"), "5-4-3-2-1" grounding using senses.

🤯When You're Overwhelmed

Sometimes, big feelings don't show up gently. They crash in. Maybe your hands shake, your stomach flips, or you just shut down completely. This is what feeling overwhelmed looks like, and if you've ever said, "I can't handle this," you're not alone. The good news? There are tools to help you stay steady, even when emotions try to knock you over.

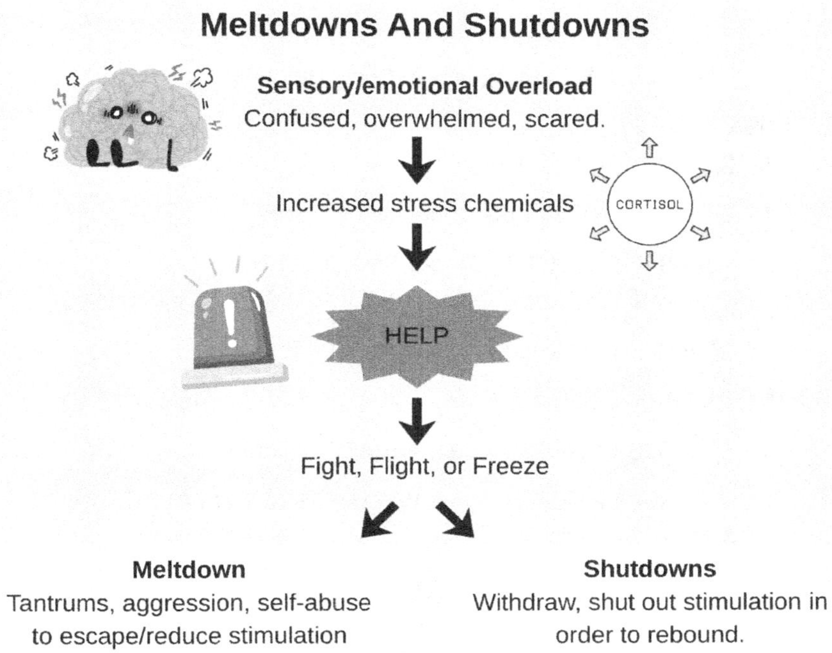

⚠ Signs You're Close to a Meltdown

Before things hit full overload, your body often gives early warning signs. You might:

- Clench your jaw
- Talk really fast or go completely silent
- Start to feel trapped, even in normal situations
- Cry without knowing exactly why
- Feel like your thoughts are racing or foggy

These signals are like yellow lights. They're telling you to slow down before things turn red. With CBT, you learn to recognize these signs early so that you can deploy techniques before the meltdown happens.

Studies have found that early emotional regulation reduces future distress among adolescents and improves coping outcomes.

📞 **Emergency & Crisis Helplines**

USA

- ☎ **911** – Emergency
- 💖 **988** – Self-harm & Crisis
- 🧠 **1-800-662-HELP** – Drugs & Mental Health

Canada

- ☎ **911** – Emergency
- 💖 **988** – Self-harm & Crisis
- 📱 **1-833-456-4566** / Text **45645** – Suicide
- 🧠 **1-866-585-0445** / Text **WELLNESS** to **741741** – Drugs & Mental Health

✋ 5-4-3-2-1 Grounding Technique

This tool is simple, science-backed, and works fast. It helps bring your attention back to the present instead of letting your brain spiral.

Here's how to try it:

- 5 things you can see (the poster on your wall, a pencil, your shoelaces...)
- 4 things you can touch (your sleeve, your desk, the floor...)
- 3 things you can hear (a clock ticking, footsteps, the AC...)
- 2 things you can smell (your shampoo, something in the kitchen...)
- 1 thing you can taste (chew gum, drink water, or just notice your mouth)

This act focuses your senses and pulls your brain out of emotional overload. Research has found that grounding techniques lower distress and boost calm, especially during anxiety spikes.

Calming Cards Activity

Let's make your own emergency kit: Calming Cards. These are index cards or digital notes with mini tools you can grab when you're overwhelmed. They might say:

- "Breathe in for 4, hold for 4, out for 4."
- "Text a friend. You don't have to feel this alone."
- "Go outside. Feel the air."
- "Play your favorite song."
- "Drink water. Reset."

Decorate them. Add stickers or doodles. Put them in a spot you'll remember: your bag, locker, or pinned above your desk. This gives your future self an assist when your brain is too swamped to think clearly.

Creating a Personal Calm Plan

Everyone's emotions work differently. That means your calm plan should fit you. Ask yourself:

- What usually helps me cool down?
- What makes things worse?
- Who can I go to when I'm spiraling?

Write it down like a mini manual. For example:
"When I feel overwhelmed, I'll…"
✔ Use my grounding technique
✔ Grab a calming card
✔ Step away and breathe
✔ Text my older cousin (she gets it)
✔ Play my "deep breath" playlist

A study in the Journal of Adolescence (Kuyken et al., 2010) found that teens who create personalized coping plans report better emotional awareness and less distress in high-pressure situations.

Permission to Feel

Sometimes we try so hard to keep it all together. Smiling when we're struggling. Saying "I'm fine" when we're anything but. But guess what? It's okay not to be okay. Feelings, especially big, messy, confusing ones, are part of being human. You don't need to push them away or fake your way through them. CBT teaches us that allowing space for emotions, instead of resisting them, is actually the healthiest choice.

I allow myself to feel happy and joyful, even when my mind is telling me otherwise.

It's Okay Not to Be Okay

You've probably heard people say, "Just stay positive," like that's supposed to fix everything. But life is not always sunshine and roses. Faking a smile when you are in pain does not make the pain go away; it just builds up so much that you feel as though you are going to explode! And sooner or later, it bubbles back up.

In fact, studies have found that accepting negative feelings without judging or avoiding them is associated with reduced distress and enhanced emotional balance long-term. Denial creates pressure. Acceptance creates peace.

The Pressure to "Be Fine" All the Time

Social media doesn't help. You scroll through highlight reels and start thinking, "Why am I the only one struggling?" You're not. Everyone has rough days, but we don't always post them.

Think about Inside Out again. Joy wanted to dominate everything, and it wasn't until Riley let Sadness take a spot in her life that she began to heal. You have permission to be joyful, sad, thrilled, and nervous; even all at the same time.

Making Space for Mixed Emotions

Have you ever felt two things at the same time? Like being proud and scared before a performance? Or feeling happy for a friend but jealous too? That's normal.

CBT calls this "both-and" thinking. It means two emotions can exist together. You can be grateful and still tired. You can love your family and still need space. And allowing yourself to feel all of it, free from guilt, can help you move through it with clarity rather than shame.

Accepting the full range of emotions rather than resisting or ignoring them predicted better psychological health and lower levels of depressive and anxiety symptoms, according to a 2017 study published in the journal Emotion.

Create a Playlist for Each Feeling

Here's a cool way to support your emotions: make a playlist for each one.

- Feeling low? Have a "Rainy Day Chill" list.
- Feeling mad? "Volume Up – Let It Out."
- Feeling nervous? "Breathe and Ground."
- Feeling hopeful? "Confidence Mode: On."

Music helps the brain regulate emotion by activating mood-processing centers like the amygdala and ventral striatum. So next time you're not sure what you feel, let your playlist speak first. Bonus: It's a gentle way to start conversations with others; just share the song.

Fun Fact

Your brain processes music using the same areas it uses for emotion regulation. That means when you listen to your favorite playlist, you're not just vibing; you're literally helping your brain calm down, focus, or feel stronger. No wonder your "Sad Bops" or "Hype Up" playlist can totally change your day!

📌Chapter Wrap-Up

Emotions aren't signs that something's wrong with you, they're signs that something matters to you. Whether it's anger that shows a boundary has been crossed, sadness that points to something important that's missing, or anxiety trying to prepare you for the unknown, each feeling has a role. You don't need to run from them or pretend they don't exist. With CBT tools, you've learned how to name emotions, track them, understand their purpose, and respond with calm and clarity instead of panic or shutdown.

You've also explored how to make your own calm-down plan, how to catch when you're near meltdown mode, and even how to make space for those tricky mixed emotions that show up out of nowhere. From mood meters to superhero comics, this chapter has shown you that emotions can be understood, and when they are, they stop feeling like enemies and start becoming allies.

Feeling and managing your emotions is one thing, but keeping your life balanced in a world full of notifications? Chapter 4 is all about mastering the social media vs. real life showdown.

🏠 Parents' Corner: Let's Think Together

💭 **Activity: "Swap the Script" Game**

- What You'll Need:
- Sticky notes or index cards
- A pen or marker
- 10 minutes together

Step 1: Teen writes down 3 negative self-talk thoughts on different notes.
Examples:

- "I always mess up."
- "I'm too sensitive."
- "No one wants to hear what I think."

Step 2: Parent flips the note and helps reframe the thought with a kinder version.
Examples:

- "Everyone messes up sometimes. I'm still learning."
- "My feelings matter, even when they're big."
- "I have ideas that deserve to be heard.

Step 3: Mix up the notes. Take turns reading one out loud and guessing: "Is this the original thought or the flipped one?"

Why it works:

It builds emotional connection, shows that reframing can be learned, and creates a safe space for real talk, without the pressure of a lecture.

🔑 Key Takeaways

- Naming your emotions helps calm your brain and shift you from reacting to responding.
- Tracking moods with color charts and journals builds self-awareness and shows helpful patterns.
- Big emotions like anger, sadness, and anxiety aren't "bad", they're messengers, not threats. CBT gives tools to recognize when you're overwhelmed and create a calm plan that works for you.
- Giving yourself permission to feel, even the hard stuff, isn't weakness. It's emotional strength.

🎧 Exercise 1: Playlist Power-Up

Music can be a secret weapon for self-belief. Build your personal power playlist.

Step 1: List songs that make you feel strong, calm, or unstoppable.

🎵 1. ______________________________

🎵 2. ______________________________

🎵 3. ______________________________

🎵 4. ______________________________

🎵 5. ______________________________

Step 2: Listen to your playlist whenever you need a confidence boost.

💭 **Reflection:** How does your energy change after listening?

✉️ Exercise 2: Talk to Your Inner Critic

Imagine your inner critic as a character — maybe grumpy, scared, or just misinformed. Write them a short letter.

Dear Inner Critic,

____

____

____

____

____

____

____

____

____

____

____

____

____

____

____

____

____

From,

Your Stronger, Kinder Self

💬 **Reflection:** What did your inner critic need to hear the most?❤️❤️

📱⚖️ CHAPTER 4:

Social Media vs. Real Life - Finding Your Balance

"Don't compare your behind-the-scenes to someone else's highlight reel.

— Steven Furtick

SOCIAL MEDIA SEEMS both a best friend and a bully at the same time. One minute, you are laughing at a video or texting with a friend. Next, you're wondering why your life doesn't look like theirs, why you weren't invited, or why your post didn't get as many likes. If you've ever felt worse after scrolling, you're not imagining it. And you're definitely not alone.

CBT (Cognitive Behavioral Therapy) teaches us how what we see impacts how we think, and how those thoughts affect how we feel. This chapter breaks tricky side of social media: the way our brains compare, judge, and respond to images and stories that are not always true. You'll discover how to spot the thought traps, challenge the comparison game, and make healthier technological habits without going totally offline.

Your Feed Isn't Reality

Scrolling through social media can feel like walking through a perfect museum; everyone's smiling, traveling, glowing. But what you're seeing isn't the full picture. It's carefully chosen, edited, and posted to show just the good stuff. Your brain might start comparing your real, messy life to their filtered highlight reel. CBT helps you catch those thoughts before they turn into beliefs, and reminds you that real life isn't curated like a feed.

Don't compare your behind-the-scenes to someone's highlight reel.

The Highlight Reel vs. Real Life

Imagine watching a movie where every single character is perfect; flawless skin, great friends, always winning. That's what most people post online: the best 2% of their lives. You rarely see the behind-the-scenes—the messy bedroom, the fight with a parent, the awkward lunch period.

But here's where CBT kicks in: your brain sees that highlight reel and starts making assumptions. "They're always happy." "Their life is better than mine." But those thoughts are not facts, just reactions to filtered moments. Studies suggest that teens who are exposed to idealized social media posts are more likely to experience negative self-perceptions, especially when it leads to upward comparison.

Try thinking like a detective again. When you see a post that stings, pause and ask: "What am I assuming right now?" "Do I really know what's going on in their life?"

Fun Fact

Instagram originally launched without filters. That's right; those sparkle-skin, warm-glow, puppy-ear effects weren't part of the plan. Filters were added *later* when developers saw how much people liked posting polished pictures.

But you know what else is true? Posts without filters now get higher engagement in some communities because they feel more *real*. Real faces. Real stories. Real connection. That's starting to trend again, and you're already ahead of it.

Filters, Edits, and Staged Content

Let's talk about filters. Not just the Instagram kind, but mental filters, too. Social media filters smooth skin, brighten eyes, and tweak angles. Mental filters, common in CBT, are when your brain only focuses on the negative about you and the positive about everyone else. That's a setup for feeling inadequate.

Remember the scene in Spider-Man: Far From Home where Mysterio creates illusions so real that Peter doubts everything? Social media can be like that: powerful illusions crafted for attention or approval. The problem isn't just that others are filtering their photos. It's that your brain forgets they are filtered.

CBT helps us catch that thinking and challenge it. Try this: the next time you find yourself scrolling and feeling low, say aloud:

"This is a moment, not the full story."

Comparing = Despairing Activity

Let's be honest: comparing yourself feels automatic. But it also creates stress, self-doubt, and mood crashes. CBT teaches that comparison often leads to distorted thinking, like all-or-nothing thoughts ("They're amazing, I'm worthless") or mind-reading ("They must think they're better than me").

Here's an activity to try:

Comparing = Despairing Journal

Make two columns. In the first, write down what you saw online that triggered comparison. In the second, write one fact that reminds you it's not the whole truth.

Example:

Scroll Trigger: "Her birthday party looked perfect."

Reality Check: "I don't know what else happened that day. I had a good hangout with my cousin."

Over time, you'll teach your brain to spot exaggerations and see yourself more fairly. Studies confirm that journaling thoughts tied to social media reduces distorted thinking and improves mood regulation.

🌱 Follow Accounts That Make You Feel Good

Your feed isn't just a reflection; it's a choice. Every time you follow someone, you're deciding what voices get airtime in your head. Ask yourself: "Does this account lift me up, teach me something, or make me feel safe?"

If not, it's okay to mute, unfollow, or take a break. That's not rude. That's healthy.

CBT supports building positive input into your daily routine. Just like choosing what music you play or what snacks you eat, you can choose content that feeds your brain in a better way. Look for accounts that talk about mental health, share real stories, or celebrate all kinds of bodies, backgrounds, and experiences.

As one teen said during a CBT session, "I started following artists and people who show their mess-ups, too. It made me feel less alone."

Likes ≠ Self-Worth 📱 ≠ 💖

It's tempting to think likes, views, and comments define your value, but they don't measure who you are. Algorithms and timing decide visibility, not your kindness, creativity, or character. CBT helps separate those two things by showing that your worth isn't tied to digital approval — it's in how you think, act, and treat yourself and others.

Your real worth comes from what you bring to life offline: being a good friend, helping family, staying true to your values, or simply showing up. If social media vanished tomorrow, those qualities would still shine. Reminding yourself of this — through journaling, affirmations, or self-reflection — helps you stop chasing validation and focus on the value you already carry..

Posting With Purpose

Let's be real: posting feels good. Sharing a funny moment, a cool outfit, or something personal can feel like opening your heart to the world. But here's the twist: posting without thinking can sometimes do the opposite. It can lead to regret, confusion, or feeling even more invisible if the response isn't what you hoped.

CBT helps us press pause before we press "post." It challenges us to consider our intention, our thoughts, and how we might feel afterward. Because every post is more than a photo; it's a message. And you deserve to know what message you're sending.

Think Before You Post (Why, Who, Impact)

Before you post anything, try asking:

- Why am I posting this?
- Who do I hope sees it?
- What might someone feel when they see it?

If your reply is, "To make people envious," or "To validate that I'm all right," then it might be worth holding off. But if it's "To express myself" or "To celebrate something that matters," you're posting from a place of strength, not comparison.

Research from the American Psychological Association shows that mindful social media use, where you reflect before sharing, leads to lower stress and more positive interactions.

Sharing Your Story With Confidence

Not every story needs to be perfect in order to be worthy of telling. Among the most powerful posts are also the most honest: "I've had a bad week, and I'm learning how to breathe," or "Here's something I created; I'm proud of it."

A million likes are not necessary to have your voice count. And even one person reading and thinking, "Me too," is enough. CBT encourages realistic expression over performance. The goal isn't applause; it's authenticity.

✨ Posting to Uplift, Not Impress

There's a huge difference between posting to connect and posting to impress. Try asking:

- "Will this help someone?"
- "Is this true to me?"
- "Do I feel okay no matter how people react?"

If your answer is yes, that's a strong post. If not, it might be coming from pressure or comparison. That's where CBT can help you rewrite the thought that says, "I have to post something perfect to feel seen."

A study in *Cyberpsychology: Journal of Psychosocial Research* on Cyberspace found that teens who use social media to support others experience higher self-esteem than those who use it primarily for image management.

✅ Social Media Intentions Checklist

Before your next post, do a quick CBT-inspired check-in:

☑ Am I sharing this because I enjoy it?
☑ Would I still like this post if no one commented?
☑ Does this reflect something real about me?
☑ Would I be okay if someone didn't agree with it?
☑ Am I okay if I don't get the response I imagined?

This little list is like a traffic light for your mind. Green light? Go ahead. Yellow light? Maybe wait and think. Red light? Save it for later, or keep it offline.

🌀 The Scroll Trap

Have you ever picked up your phone just to check one thing, and then, suddenly, 45 minutes disappear? That's the scroll trap. It starts with curiosity, then shifts to habit, and sometimes ends in exhaustion. And the more tired or bored you feel, the more you scroll.

But here's what CBT teaches: behaviors like doomscrolling don't happen randomly. They often show up when your brain is trying to escape discomfort, stress, sadness, boredom, or just plain FOMO. The trap isn't your phone, it's what your thoughts tell you while you're scrolling: "Just one more video," or "Maybe I'll feel better if I keep going."

🚨 Signs of Doomscrolling or Screen Overload

Sometimes it's obvious. Other times, it sneaks up on you. Look for these signs:

- You scroll even when you're not enjoying it
- You feel drained or anxious after using your phone
- You've re-read the same comments or watched the same stories multiple times
- You ignore other things (like sleep or homework) to keep scrolling
- You feel worse about yourself after being online

Studies found that excessive scrolling is linked to emotional numbing and mood decline, especially when teens feel out of control during use.

💥 How to Know When You Need a Break

CBT helps you check your own patterns and signals. Ask yourself:

- "Am I using my phone to avoid something hard?"
- "Did this scroll session actually make me feel better?"
- "Do I feel more connected, or more alone?"

You might even rate your mood before and after. If your "after" mood keeps dipping, that's your cue to take a pause; not as punishment, but as protection.

🔁 Replace Scrolling With Something That Helps

The goal isn't "never use your phone." The goal is to use it with awareness and give your brain better options when you're overwhelmed or bored. Try making a list of quick activities that help you reset. Here are some easy swaps:

- Instead of 20 minutes of TikTok → 5 minutes of music + a short walk
- Instead of doomscrolling the news → message a friend you trust
- Instead of watching someone else live → do one small thing that makes you feel alive (drawing, stretching, dancing in your socks)

CBT calls this "behavioral activation"—choosing actions that support your mental health rather than feed the spiral.

🧠Did You Know?

Teens who spend **more than 3 hours a day** on social media are twice as likely to report experiencing poor mental health symptoms, like anxiety or sadness, especially if they're constantly checking for feedback or comparing themselves to others.

But here's the flip: when teens **use social media intentionally** like for creative projects, supporting friends, or learning new things, they tend to feel more confident and emotionally supported. It's not about how long you're online; it's about how you use your time there.

📊 Design Your "Offline Time" Menu

Make it fun. Create a personal menu of screen-free choices. Label it: When I log off, I can:

- Play with my pet
- Do a short breathing exercise
- Write a silly poem
- Organize my desk while listening to music
- Make a snack
- Call or voice-note someone I trust

Print it. Decorate it. Post it on your wall or in your phone notes. When the scroll urge kicks in, open your menu and pick something that helps you feel better, not just busy.

⌛ Digital Detox Challenge

You don't have to go live in a cave to reset your digital habits. Even a small break can reboot your brain in big ways. That's what the digital detox challenge is all about, not quitting your phone forever, just proving to yourself that you're the one in charge of how it's used.

CBT teaches that building new habits doesn't start with pressure. It starts with awareness, small choices, and celebrating progress, not perfection.

24-Hour Phone-Free Adventure

Pick one day. Set a goal: no social apps, no doomscrolling, no mindless browsing. You can still use your phone to call or text if needed, but the idea is to disconnect from the noise.

Want to make it fun? Turn it into an adventure.

- Go on a mini hike
- Try a new recipe
- Visit a museum
- Invite a friend over for an old-school game night

Keep a notebook with you or open your phone's notes to reflect. How do you feel after an hour? After five hours? Research shows that even short-term digital detoxes can improve focus, emotional awareness, and sleep quality in teens.

📈 Track Your Screen Time + How It Makes You Feel

Sometimes we don't realize how much time we're spending online until we see it. Try this CBT-based tracking method for one week:

- Each night, check your screen time data
- Write one sentence: "How did I feel after today's screen use?"

It might say:

"Two hours on TikTok, I felt more tired than entertained."

"30 minutes messaging friends; I felt connected."

Patterns will start to pop out. And once you know them, you can change them.

🛑 Create a Digital Boundaries Plan

Just like you set a bedtime or study schedule, you can set tech boundaries. These are healthy limits you choose, not rules someone forces on you. Try writing your own:

- "I will not scroll past 10:00 p.m."
- "I will charge my phone outside my room at night."
- "I will mute accounts that stress me out."

Boundaries don't box you in; they protect your peace. A study found that teens who implemented consistent screen limits reported better mental health and self-regulation than those with no boundaries at all.

🎉 Celebrate Wins from Time Offline

Every hour you spend reconnecting with your life (instead of your feed) deserves a high-five.

- Did you get through the whole day without Instagram? Celebrate with a playlist dance party.
- Did you choose journaling instead of scrolling before bed? Mark it on your wall calendar.
- Did you silence notifications for an hour and finish your homework faster? That's a win.

CBT reminds us: reward builds habit. And you don't need anyone else's applause to know that your time is valuable.

📌Chapter Wrap-Up

Social media isn't all bad; it helps you connect, create, and express yourself. But when it starts to mess with how you see yourself or others, it's time to pause and check in. CBT helps you do just that. It teaches you to question what your brain tells you while scrolling, to notice when you're comparing or chasing validation, and to take control of your time instead of letting your feed run the show.

This chapter wasn't about deleting every app. It was about using your phone with purpose. You learned how to spot highlight reels, challenge likes-as-worth thinking, post with intention, take breaks when needed, and design a digital life that works for you, not against you.

You're not behind. You're not missing out. You're learning how to be present, and that's a win worth celebrating.

Now that you've figured out scrolling without stressing, it's time to look in the mirror, literally, and see how CBT can help you boost your self-esteem in Chapter 5.

🏠 Parents' Corner: Let's Think Together

Activity: "Offline Hour – Family Challenge"

Pick one hour this week when everyone at home unplugs. No phones. No TVs. No tablets. Just you, your family, and the real world. Set a timer. Make it fun.

Here are some quick ideas for that hour:

- Build a blanket fort and eat snacks inside.
- Go on a walk and see who can spot the weirdest cloud shape.
- Cook something simple together (microwave popcorn totally counts).
- Sit outside and make up constellations, even if it's daytime.

Reflection Questions to Ask Each Other:

- "What surprised you about not using your phone?"
- "Was anything harder or easier than you thought?"
- "Would you want to try it again?"

"Would you want to try it again?" **Teens:** You can even be the one to invite your parent to try the challenge with you. Explain it's not about rules, it's about reconnecting, together.

🔑 Key Takeaways

- Your feed is not the full story. Most posts are highlight reels, not real life.
- Likes and views don't define your value; kindness,
- CBT helps you slow down and ask "why" before you post, scroll, or compare.

- Scrolling becomes harmful when it replaces emotional needs. Replacing it with healthy behaviors can restore balance.
- You can set digital boundaries, take intentional breaks, and celebrate small wins to build habits that protect your peace.

😊 Exercise: Emoji Feelings Tracker

Emotions change like the weather — tracking them helps you spot patterns.

Step 1: Use emojis to show how you felt each day this week.

Day	Emoji	Why I Felt This Way
Monday		
Tuesday		
Wednesday		
Thursday		
Friday		
Saturday		
Sunday		

Step 2: Reflection

Which emoji showed up most often? ______

What do you think caused that pattern? ______

💡 **Tip:** There are no "bad" emotions — they're just signals waiting to be understood.

Review

If you're finding the book helpful, we'd love it if you could leave a quick review at emmadavisbooks.com
or
Amazon.com

It helps us reach more teens and the people who care about them—plus, it totally makes our day.

SCAN ME

www.emmadavisbooks.com

CHAPTER 5:

Mirror Talk - Building Self-Esteem through CBT

"You've been criticizing yourself for years, and it hasn't worked. Try approving of yourself and see what happens."

— **Louise Hay**

I USED TO THINK confidence was something you either had or didn't. But then I started noticing how often teens I worked with said things to themselves they'd never say to someone else. "I'm so stupid." "I look weird." "Why can't I be normal?" Sound familiar? You've probably had some version of those thoughts, too. This chapter is about changing that. You'll get to meet the voice in your head that keeps tearing you down, learn where it came from, and, more importantly, how to talk back. You'll also learn how to speak to yourself like you'd speak to a real friend with honesty, yes, but also with kindness. Self-esteem isn't about being perfect or always feeling amazing. It's about learning to respect yourself, even on the hard days.

Meet Your Inner Critic

Before you can change your thoughts, you need to recognize the voice that brings you down. This section helps you spot your inner critic, understand where it came from, and challenge the lies it tells. You'll learn what this voice sounds like, explore why it shows up, and take the power out of its words by naming it and treating it like a character, not a truth. Once you recognize how often it shows up, you can begin to respond differently. The goal is not to erase the voice, but to stop letting it lead.

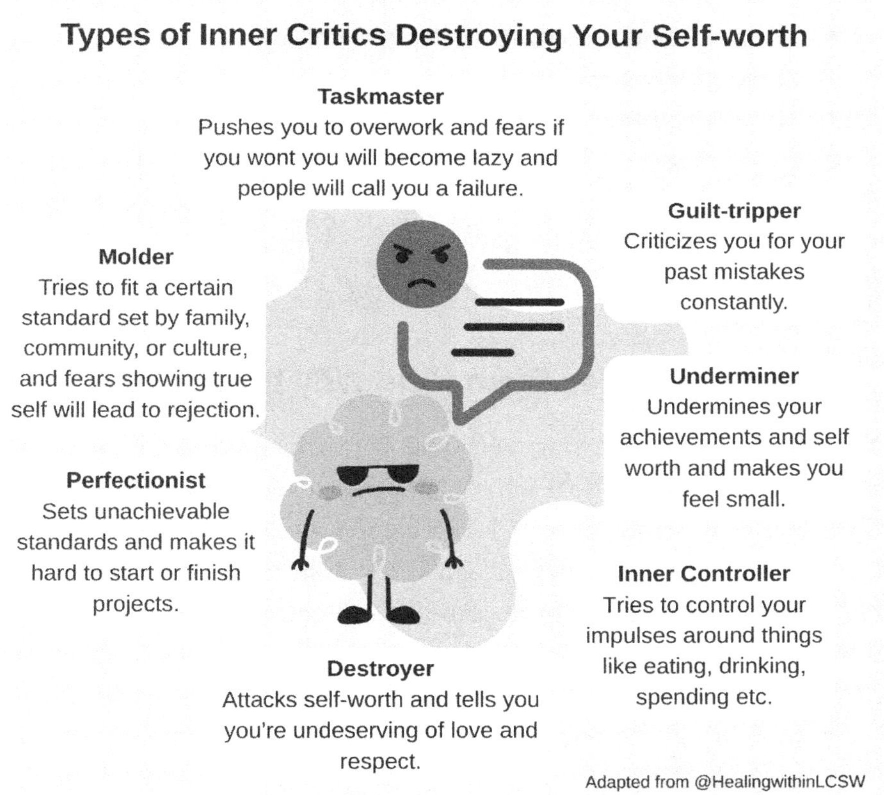

🗣️ What Your Inner Critic Sounds Like

I've heard that voice in my head, too. You know the one, it can be harsh, repetitive, and unfair. It says things that cut deep, and it always seems to show up when you're already feeling shaky. It uses absolute terms like "always" and "never," focusing on flaws instead of your effort. Unlike real feedback that helps you grow, this voice doesn't guide; it just cuts. You've probably heard things like, "You're so dumb," "You'll embarrass yourself," or "Everyone else is doing better than you." Here are some ways it might sound:

- It exaggerates mistakes
- It compares you to others unfairly
- It repeats negative phrases from the past
- It sounds louder during stress
- It tells you that you're not enough

Next time you catch yourself thinking something that makes you shrink, pause and ask: Would I say this to someone I love? If the answer is no, then it's your critic talking. That's your chance to separate truth from habit.

Where It Comes From (And Why It's Wrong)

Your inner critic didn't start with you; it was handed to you. I've seen it happen through family, teachers, media, and even random comments that were never meant to stick but somehow did. These messages pile up and slowly turn into beliefs. The critic might try to protect you from failure or embarrassment by demanding perfection, but it doesn't protect; it limits. Once you understand where it came from, you can begin to take its power away. It usually comes from experiences like:

- Childhood teasing
- Harsh discipline or shaming
- Comparisons to siblings or peers
- Messages from TV, magazines, or social media
- Pressure to succeed or be liked
- Misunderstood attempts to "motivate" you

These aren't your truths. They're echoes from moments that no longer deserve space in your mind.

🖌️ Give It a Name + Character Sketch

When I gave my inner critic a name, everything shifted. Suddenly, it wasn't me, it was a character. And that character could be challenged. When you name your critic, it loses authority. You can roll your eyes at it, laugh at it, or tell it to sit down. Humor gives you space. Creativity gives you control. When your critic becomes a whiny cartoon in a weird outfit, its insults stop sounding like facts.

Try visualizing and naming it in fun ways:

- Name it something that makes you laugh
- Picture it wearing something ridiculous
- Give it a whiny or dramatic voice
- Draw or write a short description of it
- Write out its favorite catchphrases
- Imagine it trying to boss others around, too

Your critic is just one voice, not the final word, and definitely not the truth.

🔍 Noticing When It Shows Up

Your critic is sneaky. I've caught mine whispering when I least expect it, before I try something new, after I speak up, or when I scroll through someone else's highlight reel. It doesn't always use words. Sometimes it shows up in tight shoulders, held breath, or a shaky voice. The first step is noticing it. That gives you a chance to pause, name it, and decide if it's worth listening to.

You might recognize it during:

- Sudden self-doubt before speaking
- Replaying something you said over and over
- Avoiding effort due to imagined failure
- Body tension or shallow breathing
- Hearing the same harsh words from earlier moments in life
- Feeling ashamed over small mistakes

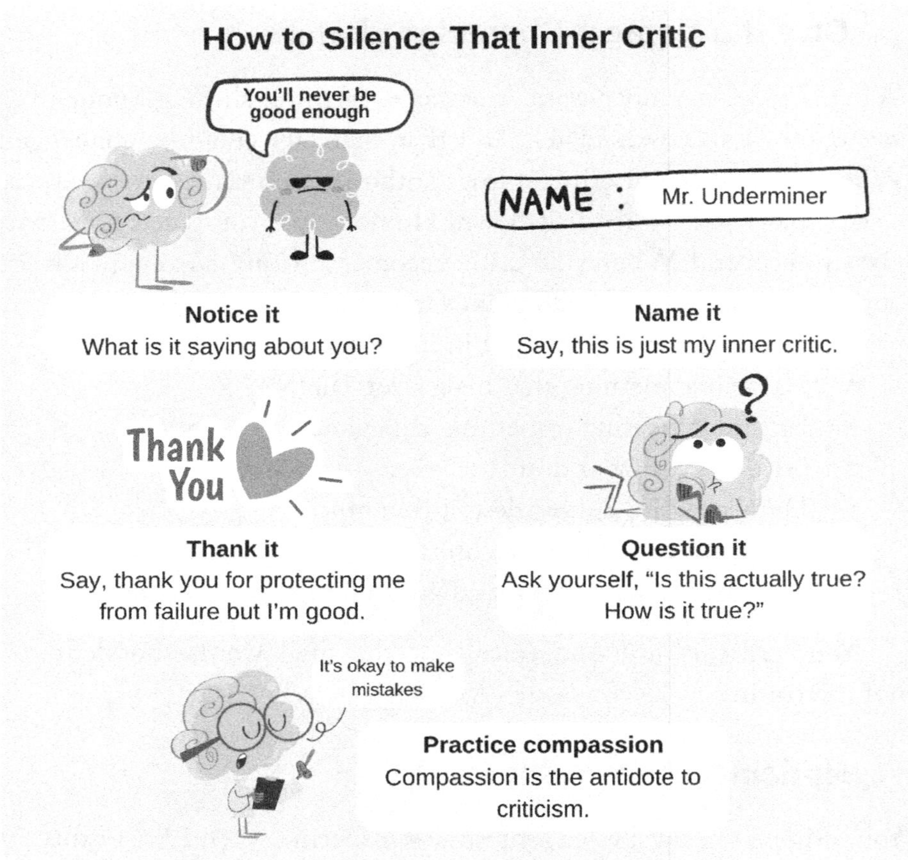

Fun Fact

Your brain releases dopamine, a feel-good chemical, when you recognize a win, no matter how small. It's the same reward signal you get from scoring in a game or receiving a like on social media. But here's the twist: you don't need anyone else to trigger it. When you track your own success, celebrate your effort, or reflect on something you're proud of, your brain reacts in the same way. That means your confidence can grow from within, not just from outside applause. In fact, people who journal small wins regularly show stronger motivation, higher self-esteem, and greater resilience.

Ask yourself: Is this voice helping or hurting me right now? The more you practice spotting it, the easier it becomes to **listen to the stronger, kinder voice inside you**.

💎 You Are More Than Your Looks

Too often, we base our value on appearance. But you are so much more than that. This section helps you break free from beauty myths and build confidence based on your character, strengths, and identity. You'll list qualities that make you valuable beyond how you look, learn to spot and challenge unrealistic media messages, and create a personal "I am" map that reflects your true worth. Your identity deserves to be built on something deeper than surface-level expectations. Let's focus on what lasts, not just what's seen.

Mirrors are just glass and you are more than that.
-r.i.d

🤓 What Makes You Valuable Besides Appearance

It's easy to forget that you are made up of so much more than what you see in the mirror. When I started focusing on my actions, values, and strengths, I noticed how much deeper my self-worth became. Beauty changes. But character, kindness, creativity, and courage, those are lasting. Your worth isn't earned through how you look. It's already there, built into who you are.

It could be things like:

- The way you treat people with respect
- Your sense of humor or quick thinking
- Your ability to bounce back from setbacks
- The courage you show when speaking up
- Your love for learning or exploring new ideas

Let yourself feel proud of who you are, not just how you appear.

Talk To Yourself 🗣️💡

Most of us speak to ourselves in ways we'd never speak to someone we care about. Shifting that inner voice toward kindness changes everything. One way to practice is by writing yourself a letter from the perspective of your best friend—encouraging, warm, and honest. Remind yourself you're trying your best, that bad days don't define you, and that you're valued for who you are, not just what you do. You can also keep a short list of self-compassion phrases like "I'm allowed to be a work in progress" or "I deserve the same kindness I give others."

When harsh thoughts creep in, practice rewriting them with balance. Instead of "I'm so lazy," try "I've had low energy today, but that doesn't make me lazy." A simple cheat sheet of positive phrases can help when your energy is low—put it somewhere visible so it's ready when you need it. The way you speak to yourself sets the tone for how you move through the world, so let your inner voice be a source of support rather than shame.

📺 Media Literacy: Unlearning Beauty Myths

The media constantly shows you filtered, edited, and unrealistic images. For a long time, I thought those images were the standard. But once

I learned how manipulated they are, I stopped comparing myself. You deserve to understand what you're up against. Unlearning these myths helps you see yourself with more clarity and more kindness. Here are some truths to remember:

- Most social media photos are edited or filtered
- Beauty standards change over time and across cultures
- Companies profit from your insecurities
- Representation in the media is still limited and biased
- No one looks like those ads all the time, not even the models

When you see an image, ask: Is this real? And if not, why should it define my worth?

List Your Non-Appearance Superpowers

What makes you powerful has nothing to do with size, skin, or shape. I once listed what I liked about myself that had nothing to do with looks, and it completely shifted my perspective. When you focus on strengths that aren't tied to appearance, you tap into a deeper kind of confidence. These are your superpowers. They make you unforgettable.

It could include strengths like:

- Empathy and deep listening
- Creative problem-solving
- Loyalty to people you care about
- Passion for a cause or subject
- Ability to stay calm under pressure
- Leading by example or standing up for others

Write these down. Revisit the list when self-image tries to shrink your shine.

🗺 "I Am..." Identity Map Activity

You are not one label. You are a whole mix of values, traits, dreams, and relationships. Creating an identity map can help you see the full picture. It shows you that even when one part feels shaky, the rest of you is still strong. This activity builds a foundation for healthy self-esteem, rooted in truth. Try mapping your identity around statements like:

- I am a learner
- I am a loyal friend
- I am creative
- I am someone who cares deeply
- I am more than one moment or one label
- I am still becoming who I want to be

Put your identity map somewhere visible. Let it remind you of who you are beyond appearance.

Did You Know?

Your brain is wired to notice mistakes more than wins. It's called the negativity bias, and it helped our ancestors survive danger but today, it can steal your confidence. That's why celebrating even small wins matters so much. Each time you write down a success, your brain starts to rewire.

Over time, consistent effort and self-recognition can help build real self-esteem not based on likes, filters, or approval from others, but from seeing your own growth in action.

Tracking progress, no matter how tiny, isn't just a feel-good idea. It's a proven mental health strategy backed by cognitive science.

🏆 Wins, Not Just Likes

Real growth isn't always visible on social media. This section focuses on tracking your personal progress, celebrating effort, and recognizing your strengths. You'll create a success journal for even the smallest victories, learn to reward yourself for trying (not just winning), and build a brag sheet filled with moments you're proud of. With help from your friends, you'll also learn how to see and believe in the strengths others already notice in you. You have more wins than you think; you need to start writing them down.

Celebrate your efforts, not just the wins, because without the efforts there are no wins.

📔 Success Journal (Even Tiny Wins Count!)

Success doesn't have to mean trophies or top grades. I've learned that some of my proudest moments were small: speaking up in class, showing up when I didn't feel like it, or calming myself during a tough moment. Start tracking those moments. When you notice them, write them down. Your brain starts to build a new habit (spotting your progress, not just your flaws).

You might include:

- I got out of bed even when I felt anxious
- I asked a question instead of pretending to understand
- I kept my cool during a tough conversation
- I remembered to take a deep breath before reacting
- I finished something I was tempted to quit

Reading back on these wins shows you how capable you are, even on the quiet days.

👏 Celebrate Effort, Not Just Outcomes

We tend to clap for results (winning the game, getting the A), but effort deserves celebration too. Think of all the times you worked hard but didn't get the "perfect" outcome. I started noticing that those moments still shaped me. Start recognizing your effort as a victory in itself. You showed up. You tried. That matters.

Ways you can celebrate effort:

- Write a note to yourself after trying something brave
- Share your process with a friend who gets it
- Treat yourself to something small when you finish a hard task
- Reflect on what you learned, even if it didn't go as planned
- Acknowledge your progress out loud, even if no one else does

Rewarding effort keeps your motivation alive, even when results take time.

📜 Brag Sheet: List 10 Things You're Proud Of

You don't have to wait for someone else to recognize your worth. I made a brag sheet once and was shocked at how many things I'd downplayed. You can do this too. Make a list of ten things you've done that you're proud of. Big or small. Don't judge (just write).

Here are a few types of wins to think about:

- Times you helped someone without being asked
- Moments you spoke up for yourself or others
- Skills you've learned or improved
- Obstacles you've overcome
- Personal rules you stuck to when it was hard
- Kindnesses you've shown to yourself

Look at your brag sheet when self-doubt creeps in. It's proof of your strength.

Strength Spotting with Friends

Sometimes we miss our own strengths, but friends see what we overlook. I've done this exercise with teens, and it's powerful. Pair up and name what you admire in each other (not surface stuff, but the real strengths). You can also ask a few trusted people: "What's one thing you think I'm good at?" Things friends might say:

- You stay calm when things get messy
- You always notice when someone's left out
- You're creative and think outside the box
- You make people feel safe and heard
- You stand up for what you believe in

Write down what they share. Then read it like a mirror. This is you, even when you forget it.

Confidence Boosters

Activity	What to Do	Why It Helps
Try Something New and Reflect	Step into something unfamiliar—join a club, speak up in class, ask a question, or try a hobby as a beginner. Afterwards, write about how it felt and what you learned.	Each new experience stretches your comfort zone and proves to your brain you can handle challenges, turning small acts of bravery into lasting confidence.

Activity	What to Do	Why It Helps
Power Pose Practice	Stand tall with feet hip-width apart, hands on hips, chin lifted. Breathe deeply and hold the pose for two minutes before a stressful event.	Posture influences mindset. Power poses help you feel grounded and prepared, activating confidence rather than faking it.
Create Your Hype Playlist	Build a playlist of songs that energize you—dance tracks, bold lyrics, music tied to strong memories, or beats that make you move. Play it when you need a lift.	Music taps into energy and emotion, helping you shift mood and reconnect with your strength quickly.
One Daily Compliment Challenge	Give yourself one genuine compliment each day, spoken out loud or written down. Focus on effort, growth, or kindness.	Trains your brain to notice strengths instead of flaws, building a more supportive inner voice over time.

📌Chapter Wrap-Up

Self-esteem doesn't grow from perfection or pretending everything's fine. It grows from how you respond to yourself, especially when things are hard. This chapter helped you do just that. You met your inner critic, gave it a name, and started to recognize when it shows up. More importantly, you began learning how to talk back, not with more shame, but with honesty and self-respect.

You practiced treating yourself like a friend, rewriting old patterns of harsh thoughts, and using tools like positive self-talk and identity maps to build a steadier view of who you are. You stopped letting your appearance define your worth and started seeing your strengths in how you think, care, and show up. You learned that confidence wasn't something you had to wait for. It was something you practiced by trying new things, using body language, curating energy through music, and speaking kindly to yourself, one compliment at a time.

This chapter reminded you that how you speak to yourself matters. And you're learning to speak with courage, not cruelty. That's a strength. That's growth. And it's already inside you.

With your confidence leveling up, the next challenge is finding calm in the chaos, so get ready for some mindfulness magic in Chapter 6.

🏠 Parents' Corner: Let's Think Together

Activity: "Self-Talk Swap – One Week Check-In"

For one week, each family member keeps track of one negative thought they catch themselves thinking. At the end of the week, come together to share what those thoughts were and how you reworded them into something more encouraging. This isn't about being perfect. It's about practicing self-kindness together.

Here are a few ways to start the swap:

- Turn "I'm not good at this" into "I'm still learning."
- Change "I always mess up" to "Mistakes help me grow."
- Try "No one likes me" as "I'm still finding my people."
- Switch "I'm so weird" into "I'm uniquely me."

Reflection Questions to Ask Each Other:

- "What negative thought showed up the most for you?"
- "How did it feel to reword it in a kinder way?"

- "What's one self-kind thing someone said to you this week?"

Teens: Invite your parent to join you in this self-talk challenge. It might surprise you how much grown-ups need to reframe their thoughts, too.

Key Takeaways

- Your inner critic is not the truth. It's a habit of thought shaped by past voices, not your present reality.
- Talking to yourself like a friend builds self-respect and quiets shame-based thinking.
- You are more than your looks. Strength, kindness, curiosity, and courage are all part of your worth.
- Noticing your wins, no matter how small, helps retrain your brain to see progress instead of failure.
- Confidence grows through practice. Trying new things, using your body language, and affirming your efforts help you build it from the inside out.

Exercise 1: Coping Menu

Create your own coping menu with strategies in three categories: appetizers (quick fixes), main courses (long-term strategies), and desserts (treats).

Appetizers (Quick Fixes):

Main Courses (Long-Term Strategies):

Desserts (Treats/Rewards):

CHAPTER 6:

Mindfulness in a Noisy World - Finding Your Calm with CBT

"You can't stop the waves, but you can learn to surf."

– Jon Kabat-Zinn

SOME DAYS OUR brains feel like a crowded hallway between classes, full of noise, movement, and a hundred things pulling at our attention. When that happens, you and I can step to the side, lean against a quiet wall, and take a deep breath. That is what mindfulness feels like. It is not about clearing our minds completely or trying to become a Zen monk. It is about noticing what is happening right now and letting it be, without getting swept away. You and I have probably done it before without even realizing it. Maybe we stared at the clouds after school, listened to a favorite song with our eyes closed, or focused on the taste of that first bite of pizza. Mindfulness is simply learning how to do that on purpose so we can find calm even when life around us gets loud.

What Even Is Mindfulness?

Sometimes I catch myself rushing through the day like I'm on autopilot, half-listening, half-thinking, half-everything. You've probably had those moments too. Mindfulness is the opposite of that. It's choosing to slow down and really notice what's going on inside and around you. It's not about clearing your mind or pretending things are perfect. It's about being present, without judging what you're feeling or trying to fix it. When we practice mindfulness, we're just giving ourselves permission to pause, breathe, and actually be here for our own lives. The more we do it, the easier it gets, and the calmer we feel, even when things get loud or messy.

🧠 A Simple Definition You Can Actually Use

Mindfulness is you and me choosing to show up for the moment we're in. That's it. We don't try to change it or run from it. We just notice. I think of it like pressing a pause button in my brain so I can really see, feel, and hear what's happening. You might think of it like this:

- Pressing pause on autopilot thoughts
- Noticing instead of reacting
- Being awake instead of just getting through

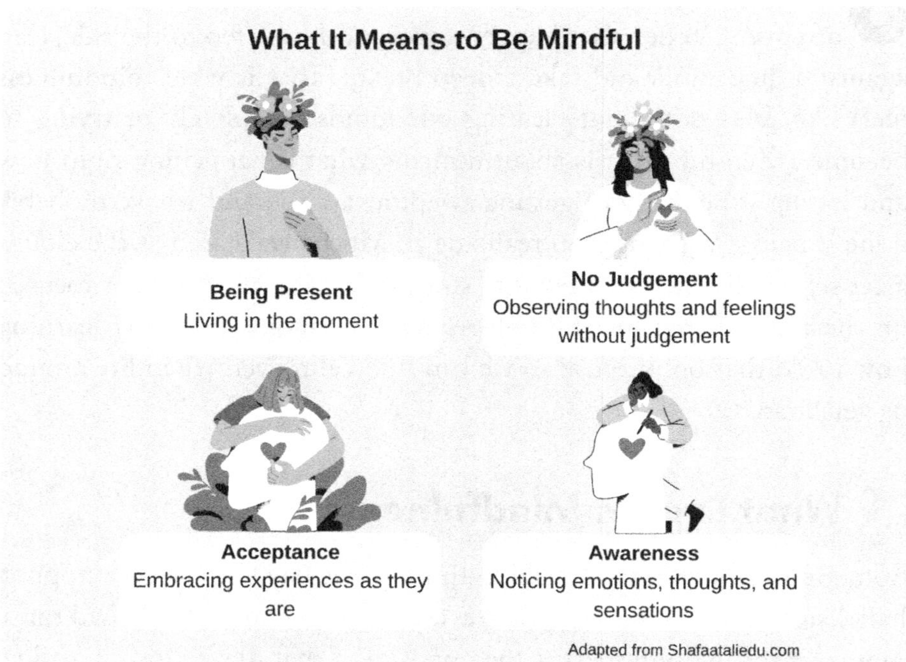

When you're walking, feel your feet hit the ground. When you're eating, actually taste each bite. When you're talking to someone, listen without already planning your response. That's mindfulness. It's not fancy, it's just being here. And honestly? It feels kind of powerful.

Mindfulness vs. Zoning Out

Here's the thing. Sometimes I stare at my screen and realize I've read the same sentence five times. I'm physically there, but mentally I'm somewhere else. That's zoning out. And we all do it.

Mindfulness is different. It's when we choose to stay connected, to ourselves, to the moment, to what's real. Here's the difference:

- **Zoning out:** Mind gone, body still here
- **Mindfulness:** Mind and body are both here together
- **Zoning out:** You miss the moment
- **Mindfulness:** You live in the moment

When you're mindful, you notice stuff you usually miss, like the sound of birds outside, the warmth of sunlight on your face, or the way your shoulders relax when you exhale. You catch the little things that make life feel more alive.

You've Already Done This, You Just Didn't Know It

Chances are, you've been mindful before without even trying. I have too. Think about moments like these:

- Watching a sunset and feeling still
- Listening to your favorite song and getting chills
- Eating something delicious and slowing down to savor it
- Laughing with friends and forgetting about your phone

Those moments are mindfulness. That's you being fully present, even just for a few seconds. Your mind wasn't jumping ahead or rewinding the past. It was just here. And you can create more moments like that on purpose.

I've found that the more I practice, the more grounded I feel. Less stressed. More me.

🍎 Try This: Eat a Snack Mindfully

Let's try something simple. Grab a snack, anything you like. A grape, a cracker, a piece of chocolate. Got it? Now slow down.

1. **Look at it.** Notice the color, shape, and texture.
2. **Smell it.** Take a slow breath. What does it smell like?
3. **Touch it.** Feel it in your fingers. Is it smooth? Bumpy?
4. **Taste it.** Take a small bite. Let the flavor roll around your tongue.
5. **Listen.** Does it crunch or squish? What do you hear?

As you eat, try to stay with the experience. If your mind wanders (and it will), just gently bring it back. No pressure. No judgment.

I do this when I need a reset, and it helps me feel more grounded, like I've returned to myself. Try it and see how it feels. You can use the same idea when you walk, brush your teeth, or even take a deep breath between classes.

🎯 Tune In to Right Now

Sometimes my mind feels like it's jumping in five different directions, and I don't even realize I've left the present moment. You might feel that way too, especially when you're stressed, distracted, or overwhelmed. That's why grounding ourselves right now matters. It helps us come back to our bodies, our breath, and our surroundings. These simple techniques help you slow down, notice what's real, and feel more steady.

🍀 The 5 Senses Grounding Technique

When I need to calm down fast, I use this grounding trick. It brings me back to the present moment by helping me focus on my senses. You can try it too, anytime your thoughts feel too loud. Here's how to do it:

- Name five things you can see
- Name four things you can touch
- Name three things you can hear
- Name two things you can smell
- Name one thing you can taste

This simple routine helps me feel more aware of what's around me and less stuck in my head. It can do the same for you.

⏳ What It Means to Be Present

Being present means I'm really here, not stuck in yesterday or racing toward tomorrow. You've probably felt this before. Maybe when you were watching a sunset, laughing with a friend, or lost in a great song, in those moments, you weren't overthinking. You were just there.

It's not about clearing your mind. It's about paying attention without judgment. When I'm present, I feel more grounded and more like myself. And when you practice being present, even in small ways, life starts to feel a little more real and a lot less rushed.

You can be present when you:

- Feel your feet hit the ground while walking

- Listen fully to someone without planning your reply
- Notice your breath instead of rushing past it

Presence is a practice. Every moment is a new chance to try it.

🩺 Breathing Bubbles or Box Breathing

When I feel anxious or tense, I come back to my breath. You can too. It's something you always have with you, and it can help calm your mind in just a few seconds. One of my favorite ways is box breathing.

Try this pattern:

- Inhale for 4 seconds
- Hold for 4 seconds
- Exhale for 4 seconds
- Hold for 4 seconds

Imagine tracing the sides of a box with your breath. You can also picture a gentle breathing bubble that grows as you breathe in and shrinks as you breathe out. Some people like using breathing bubble videos. I sometimes just imagine it in my head. Either way, it's a powerful tool to slow down and reset.

👁 Describe Your Surroundings Without Judgment

Sometimes my thoughts get loud, or I start feeling anxious without knowing why. When that happens, I stop and start describing what's around me, not with opinions, just with observations. You can try this too. It helps you come back to the moment.

Look around and say what you notice. Not whether you like it or not, just what it is. You might describe things like:

- "The chair is gray and has a soft cushion."
- "The window is open a little."
- "I hear a car passing outside."
- "There's a slight breeze against my arm."

This helps shift your brain from overthinking to simply noticing. The more you do it, the easier it gets to stay calm, even when things feel uncertain.

Fun Fact

Your brain and body respond quickly when you focus on the present moment. Techniques like mindful breathing or using your five senses help calm your nervous system by lowering cortisol, the stress hormone. In fact, studies show that just one minute of grounding or deep breathing can slow your heart rate and improve focus. It's like hitting a reset button in your brain. Being present doesn't just feel good; it helps your body find balance and calm.

Calm Your Inner Chaos

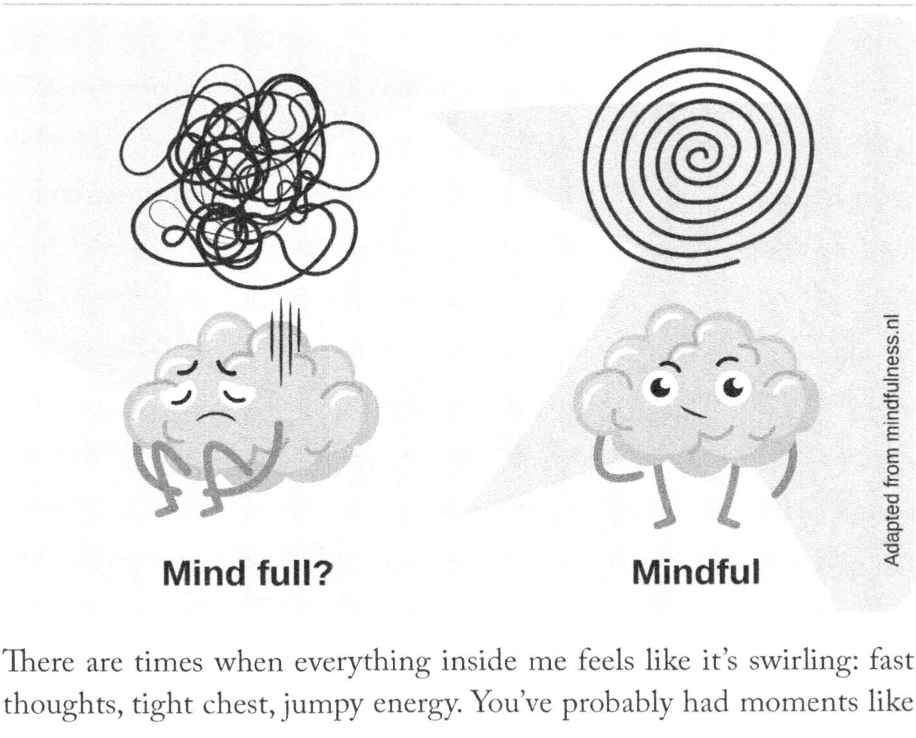

There are times when everything inside me feels like it's swirling: fast thoughts, tight chest, jumpy energy. You've probably had moments like that, too. Whether it's stress about school, people, or just life being too much, it can feel hard to get a grip. Mindfulness is like hitting the slow-motion button. It doesn't fix everything, but it gives you a way to step back and breathe through it. Instead of getting pulled into the chaos, you learn how to notice it, feel it, and still stay steady.

Why Mindfulness Helps with Stress and Anxiety

When I feel anxious, my brain wants to either run away from the feeling or fix everything all at once. You've probably been there too. But mindfulness teaches us something different. It invites us to slow down, stay present, and sit with the emotion without judging or panicking.

Instead of spiraling, I remind myself that emotions are temporary. They rise, peak, and pass just like waves. And I don't have to fight them. I can ride them.

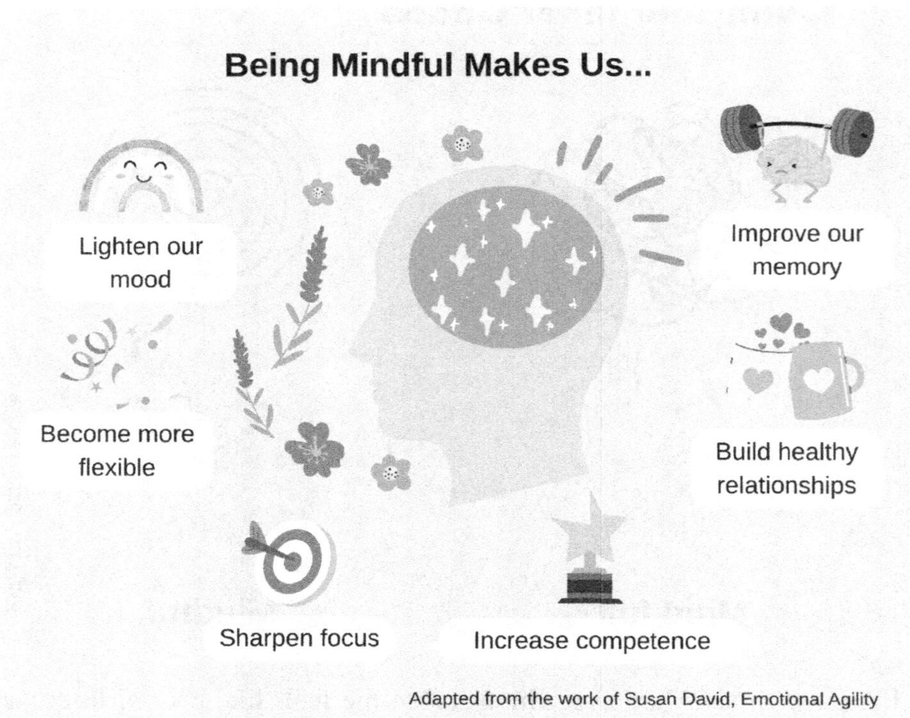

Mindfulness helps your body and brain calm down. When you breathe deeply, name what you're feeling, or pause before reacting, you send your nervous system a message: "You're safe."

Try these when you're overwhelmed:

- Pause, breathe in slowly, and say: "This feeling will pass."
- Put your hand on your heart and notice its rhythm.
- Feel your feet on the ground and say, "I'm here."

It really helps.

📔 Journaling Your Stormy vs. Calm Moments

One thing that's helped me a lot is writing down what I feel. I don't worry about grammar or being deep. I just let the thoughts spill out. You can do this too.

Try journaling about a time you felt stormy. What was going on in your body? What thoughts were racing? Then, write about a moment when you felt calm and safe. What helped? What did your body feel like?

Here's a journaling prompt to try:

- "Right now, I feel..."
- "The storm inside me sounds like..."
- "The calm feels like..."

This practice helps you notice your patterns and gives you clues about what truly grounds you.

Nature Walks and Mindful Movement

Sometimes when I'm overwhelmed, sitting still doesn't help. I need to move, to walk, stretch, dance, or just shake things out. Movement shifts energy, and it can shift your mood, too. You might feel the same.

When things feel tight or heavy, I go outside and walk slowly. I pay attention to the ground under my feet, the color of the trees, the sounds around me, and the rhythm of my breath. I don't rush. I just move.

Mindful movement isn't about burning calories. It's about tuning in instead of zoning out. Your body already knows how to release tension. You just have to listen.

Try one of these simple resets:

- Stretch your arms up and take a deep breath
- Dance to a favorite song, eyes closed
- Walk barefoot for a minute and notice how it feels

Let your body lead.

Did You Know?

When you're overwhelmed, your brain shifts into survival mode. This is called the fight, flight, or freeze response, and it's your body's way of trying to protect you. The problem is, your brain doesn't always know the difference between real danger and everyday stress like homework or social pressure.

Mindfulness helps calm that stress response. When you pause, breathe deeply, or name what you're feeling, your brain starts to shift out of panic mode and into a calmer, more focused state. That's not just a vibe, it's neuroscience.

Studies show that even a few minutes of mindfulness a day can lower anxiety, improve sleep, and increase emotional resilience. You're not just chilling out. You're retraining your brain to handle life with more clarity and calm.

Build a Calm-Down Corner

When the world feels too loud, I like having a space that feels like mine. You can create a calm-down corner anywhere: a small part of your room, a blanket fort, or even just a pillow and journal in a quiet spot.

It's not about having something perfect. It's about having somewhere to go when your emotions feel too big.

Your calm space might include:

- A soft blanket or pillow

- A journal or sketchbook
- Calming scents like lavender
- A favorite quote or photo
- Headphones and a playlist that soothes you

Whenever life feels too much, that space can be your reset. You're allowed to pause. You're allowed to take care of yourself.

Practice, Not Perfect

Mindfulness isn't about getting it right every time. It's about showing up, even when your thoughts are noisy or your focus feels off. I used to think I had to be perfectly still or peaceful to "do it right," but that pressure only made me feel worse. Once I let go of that idea, I found more freedom. You can too. This section is about making space for imperfect practice and learning to trust the process.

💥 It's Okay If Your Brain Wanders

If your thoughts start racing during meditation or you keep forgetting to stay mindful, that doesn't mean you're doing it wrong. It means you're human. I used to get annoyed with myself every time I got distracted, but then I realized the moment I notice I've wandered is the moment I'm being mindful again. That's a win.

So when your brain jumps around, don't judge it. Just gently guide your attention back to your breath, your senses, or the present moment. This isn't about clearing your mind completely. It's about coming back again and again with kindness. Try these gentle reminders:

- Notice when you've drifted
- Bring your attention back softly
- Let go of judgment
- Keep practicing with patience

You'll have days where mindfulness feels effortless, and other days where it doesn't. Both are part of the journey. The more you practice letting go of judgment, the more peace you'll find. Keep practicing, not to be perfect, but to be present with whatever shows up.

Apps, Music, and Meditations

Your phone doesn't have to add stress—it can support your calm. Mindfulness isn't just sitting in silence; it can be listening to a chill playlist, trying a meditation app, or pausing to breathe. Teen-friendly apps like Headspace, Smiling Mind, Insight Timer, Calm, and Breathe make it easy to slow down or fall asleep. Music works too: create a playlist with lo-fi, piano, or nature sounds that feel like an exhale.

You can also experiment with guided vs. silent mindfulness. Guided sessions give structure, while silent moments help you tune into yourself. Start small with a 3-minute meditation: sit, breathe, and gently bring your focus back when it drifts. Even short practices build a habit of calm you can carry into your day.

Mindful Habits You Can Sneak into Your Day

You don't have to stop everything to practice mindfulness. Some of my favorite moments happen when I just pause during something I'm already doing. You can sneak mindfulness into your day without adding anything extra to your schedule. Try these everyday mindful habits:

- Brush your teeth while noticing the texture and taste
- Eat a snack slowly, paying attention to each bite
- Walk with awareness of how your feet touch the ground
- Take five deep breaths before opening a message
- Look up at the sky and really see it

These habits bring you back to the now. You don't have to sit cross-legged or light candles. Just choose one small thing to do with your full attention.

📊 Weekly Reflection: When Did I Feel Most Present?

At the end of each week, I like to ask myself, "When did I feel most present?" It helps me notice what grounds me and what pulls me away. You can do this too. You don't need a fancy journal. Just take a quiet minute on Sunday night or whenever you unwind.

Reflect on your week:

- When did time feel slow or still?
- What activities helped you feel calm?
- Who were you with when you felt grounded?
- What made you feel most alive or connected?

This kind of reflection builds self-awareness. It's not about fixing anything. It's about paying attention to what fills you up. Once you notice those moments, you can start creating more of them.

Story Time: A Mindful Moment on the Basketball Court

I remember one afternoon at school, right before a big exam, my brain was buzzing. My heart was racing, and I felt like I couldn't focus on anything. So I grabbed a basketball and went out to the empty court. I wasn't playing hard, just gently bouncing the ball, listening to its rhythm, watching it rise and fall. I noticed the warm sun on my back, the sound of the rubber hitting the pavement, and the way my breath slowed down.

For those few minutes, I wasn't thinking about the test or anything else. I was just there. Breathe. Bounce. Repeat. It was the first time I realized mindfulness didn't have to look like sitting still with my eyes closed. It could be moving, noticing, and letting go.

That tiny moment helped me feel calm, and I carried that feeling with me into the rest of my day.

📌Chapter Wrap-Up

Mindfulness isn't about getting it perfect. It's about coming back, again and again, with patience. In this chapter, you gave yourself permission to pause, reflect, and show up more fully. You learned that presence doesn't mean shutting out the world. It means meeting your thoughts, feelings, and body with attention, not judgment.

You practiced simple habits like breathing when your mind wandered, tuning in instead of zoning out, and gently returning to the moment. You explored the difference between being consistent and being intense, and you noticed how tiny habits, done with care, can shift your whole day. You didn't need to "clear your mind" or be still for hours. You just needed to notice. That is mindfulness.

After learning how to tune into your own mind, it's time to tune into others. Chapter 7 will show you how to talk it out, set boundaries, and communicate like a pro.

🏠 Parents' Corner: Let's Think Together

Activity: "Mindful Moments Map"

For five days, you and your teen each write down one mindful moment from your day. It can be anything, such as a deep breath before reacting, really tasting your food, or noticing a sunset. At the end of the week, share your lists together.

Examples of mindful moments:

- I paused and took three slow breaths before answering an upsetting message.
- I noticed the way the sunlight hit the floor in the kitchen.
- I listened to a full song without checking my phone.
- I chose not to multitask while eating lunch.

Reflection Questions to Ask Each Other:

- "What made that moment feel mindful to you?"
- "Did anything surprise you about being present?"
- "How did it feel to slow down, even for a second?

Key Takeaways

- It's okay if your mind wanders. Mindfulness means noticing, not forcing silence.
- Small, steady habits are more powerful than rare, intense efforts.
- You can add mindfulness to ordinary moments like brushing your teeth or walking to class.
- Reflection helps you understand what grounds you and when you feel most alive.
- You don't need to be "good at mindfulness." You just need to come back.

Exercise 1: Mirror Talk

Say one kind thing to yourself in the mirror every day for a week. Please write it down after you say it.

Day 1: ____________________

Day 2: ____________________

Day 3: ____________________

Day 4: ____________________

Day 5: ____________________

Day 6: ____________________

Day 7: ____________________

Exercise 2: Fear-Facing Map

Draw a map of your "fear zones" and "brave zones." Then, pick one fear to step into and reflect on the experience.

My Fear Zones:

My Brave Zones:

The Fear I Chose to Step Into:

Reflection (What happened, how I felt, what I learned):

CHAPTER 7:

Talk It Out - Relationships, Boundaries, and Communication

"The way we communicate with others and with ourselves ultimately determines the quality of our lives."

– Tony Robbins

I USED TO THINK I had to keep quiet to keep the peace. Maybe you've felt that way, too. But I've learned that real connection doesn't come from silence or pretending everything's okay. It comes from learning how to speak up, how to listen, and how to respect yourself and others at the same time. In this chapter, you and I are going to explore what makes a relationship feel safe, how to set boundaries without guilt, and how to handle conflict without blowing up or shutting down. Communication isn't about being perfect. It's about being real, even when it's hard. So if you've ever struggled to say no, to express what you need, or to walk away from something that hurts, this is your space to learn, reflect, and grow.

What Makes a Healthy Relationship?

When it comes to relationships, the most important lesson I've learned is this: how you feel around someone matters more than what they say. Real connection isn't about constant excitement or fitting into someone's mold. It's about being accepted for who you already are. This section will explore how to spot the good, notice the bad, and reflect on your relationships in a way that builds trust, not confusion.

Friendship Green Flags

You can tell a lot about a relationship by how calm or tense your body feels in it. Healthy friendships have a few signs that show things are safe and supportive. I call those "green flags." These are the moments that make you feel like you can breathe easier. They may seem small, but they matter a lot.

- They check in on you, even when they don't need anything
- You laugh easily and feel more energized after hanging out
- They celebrate your wins without competition
- You can be quiet or weird without being judged

A real friend doesn't make you question your worth. They don't keep score or pull away when you shine. When you notice these green flags, pay attention. It means your relationship has the kind of foundation that can last. Start collecting moments like these. They're worth more than flashy words or big gestures.

⚠️ How to Tell If Something's Off

Sometimes, something feels "off," but you can't explain it. I've learned not to ignore that gut feeling. Your body often notices things before your mind does. Relationships shouldn't make you feel small, anxious, or like you're always apologizing. It's okay to name when something feels wrong.

- You leave the conversation feeling drained or unsure
- You stop being honest because it feels risky
- You're walking on eggshells or overthinking your texts
- You give more than you get, constantly

You don't need a dramatic reason to question a relationship. If someone makes you feel less like yourself, that's reason enough. Ask yourself: Do I feel safe? Heard? Respected? If the answer is no, take it seriously. You're allowed to protect your peace. It's not rude or selfish to want relationships that nourish you instead of wear you down.

🌱 Relationship Reflection Activity

Sometimes, it's hard to tell if a relationship is helping or hurting. That's where reflection comes in. I started asking myself questions, not to judge anyone, but to see clearly. When you get honest with yourself, things become easier to sort out. Try this activity when you want clarity.

- Think of one relationship in your life right now.
- Ask yourself: How do I feel before, during, and after spending time with them?
- What do I trust them with, and what do I hide?
- Do I like who I am around them?

Write your answers in a journal or notes app. No one else has to read it. This is just for you. When you take time to reflect, you get to know what feels right and what needs to shift. That's where real growth begins, not just in the relationship, but in you.

Fun Fact

Did you know your brain releases oxytocin, often called the "bonding hormone," when you feel safe and connected to someone? It's the same chemical that boosts trust and lowers stress levels. That means healthy relationships aren't just emotionally supportive; they help your brain and body feel more balanced. On the flip side, tense or toxic relationships can increase cortisol, the stress hormone. So when a friendship leaves you feeling calm and accepted, it's more than just a feeling; it's backed by brain chemistry.

Setting Boundaries Without Guilt

Setting boundaries isn't about being mean or shutting people out. It's about choosing peace, safety, and honesty in your relationships. I used to feel guilty for needing space or saying no. But boundaries aren't walls. They're doors. You get to decide who comes in, how close they get, and what behavior is welcome. This section will help you understand what boundaries really are and how to set them without guilt or fear.

What Boundaries Actually Are

A boundary is a clear way of saying what works for you and what doesn't. You might think of it as a line, but I like to imagine it as a signal. It tells others how to treat you, and it teaches you how to protect your own peace.

- A boundary is saying no without apology
- A boundary is asking for space when you need it
- A boundary is turning off your phone to rest
- A boundary is choosing not to explain everything

You don't need a big reason to set one. Feeling overwhelmed, disrespected, or ignored is reason enough. The more you practice, the easier it gets. And you'll start to feel stronger, not mean. You're not here to be available to everyone all the time. You're here to be true to yourself.

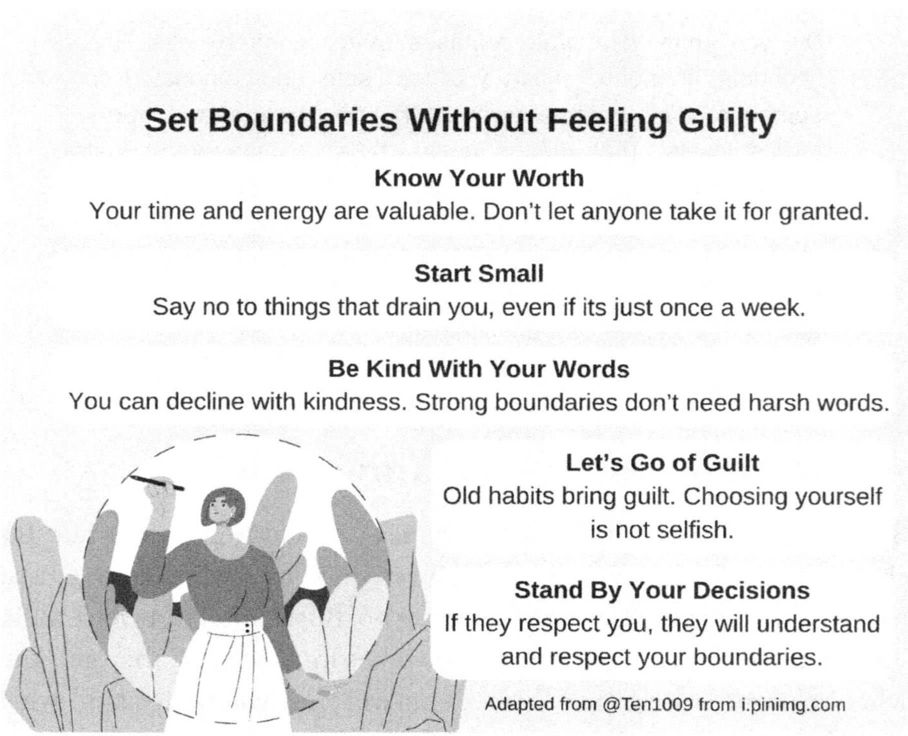

🗣️ Scripts for Saying No or Asking for Space

Saying no can feel awkward. I used to freeze or over-explain. But the truth is, you can be kind and firm at the same time. Practicing simple phrases can help. Scripts give you something to lean on when you're nervous or unsure.

- "I care about you, but I need some time alone right now."
- "I'm not up for talking about that today."
- "Thanks for asking, but I'll pass."
- "I need space to think. Let's talk later."

You don't owe people long explanations. If someone respects you, they'll understand or at least try to. If they don't, that's useful information too. Start with small boundaries and build from there. Your voice deserves to be heard, and your energy deserves to be protected.

🙅‍♂️ Know Your Personal Deal-Breakers

Everyone has a line they shouldn't have to cross. Those are your deal-breakers, and naming them helps you stay grounded. You don't have to wait for something big to happen. You can decide ahead of time what you're not okay with. That's how you keep yourself safe and strong.

- Lying or hiding important things
- Ignoring your boundaries repeatedly
- Making you feel guilty for saying no
- Controlling your time, body, or choices
- Speaking to you with disrespect or sarcasm

Make your own list. Think about what drains you or makes you feel small. Your deal-breakers aren't up for debate. If someone can't respect them, it's okay to step back. You're not being dramatic. You're being honest about what helps you thrive.

Draw Your Boundary Bubble

Sometimes it helps to visualize your boundaries. I like to picture a bubble around me: soft but strong. I decide what gets through and what bounces off. This isn't about shutting people out. It's about letting in what feels safe and loving. Try this:

- Close your eyes and imagine a clear bubble around your body
- Picture the people, words, and energy that feel safe inside
- Imagine harmful or draining things gently bouncing off
- Take a deep breath and say to yourself: I protect my space

This exercise might seem small, but it trains your mind to notice what supports you. The more clearly you define your bubble, the easier it becomes to speak up and step away when needed. You're allowed to take up space and protect it.

⚖️ Conflict Management

Step	Why it Matters	How to Do It
Face It	Avoiding builds tension and resentment.	Speak up instead of staying silent.
Use "I"	Keeps things calm and less defensive.	"I feel hurt when I'm left out."
Rewrite	Swap blame for honesty.	"You never listen." → "I feel unheard when interrupted."
Cool Down	Prepares you to talk clearly.	Walk, breathe, write, or pause before speaking.

🗣️ Speaking Up With Confidence

You deserve to be heard. Speaking up isn't about being the loudest voice in the room. It's about saying what you really mean without shrinking or exploding. I used to think I had to stay quiet to keep things peaceful, but I was holding myself back. You don't need to be rude or overly nice.

You can be clear, honest, and respectful at the same time. Here's how to build that kind of voice.

🧭 How to Say What You Mean

Saying what you mean starts with knowing what you feel. If you're unclear inside, it's hard to speak clearly outside. I've learned to pause, check in, and then speak from that place of truth. Use these steps:

- Pause before reacting
- Ask yourself, "What do I really need right now?"
- Keep your message short and simple
- Say it calmly, even if it feels scary
- Let go of how they'll react. You're being honest.

It's okay if your voice shakes. What matters is that you're showing up for yourself. You're allowed to ask for what you need, express when something hurts, or just share your thoughts. Speaking clearly builds stronger relationships and helps people see the real you.

⚖️ Assertive vs. Passive vs. Aggressive

There are different ways people speak in tough situations. Knowing the difference helps you choose how you want to show up. I used to swing between staying silent (passive) and snapping (aggressive). But the goal is to be assertive.

Here's how they compare:

- Passive: You don't say what you want. You feel small or ignored
- Aggressive: You speak loudly or harshly. Others feel hurt or defensive
- Assertive: You speak clearly and kindly. You respect yourself and the other person
- Assertive means being direct, respectful, and calm
- It says, "I matter, and so do you."

When you're assertive, you're not trying to win or avoid. You're aiming for honesty and balance. That kind of voice builds trust and shows strength, not weakness.

✋ Body Language and Tone Practice

How you say something can matter even more than the words. Your body and tone send a message, too. When I started paying attention to my posture and voice, people began listening more closely. Practice these habits:

- Stand or sit tall. Don't shrink
- Look the person in the eyes, even briefly
- Speak at a steady, clear pace
- Keep your face relaxed instead of tense
- Avoid crossing your arms or looking away too much

You can even rehearse in the mirror or record yourself. It might feel awkward at first, but confidence grows with practice. You're not trying to perform. You're trying to connect. The way you carry yourself can help people take you seriously and help you take yourself seriously, too.

🚪 When It's Time to Walk Away

Not every relationship is meant to last. Some start out great but grow heavy over time. I've stayed in friendships too long, hoping things would get better. But deep down, I knew something wasn't right. Walking away doesn't mean you failed. It means you're protecting your peace. You don't have to stay loyal to pain. If a relationship drains you more than it lifts you, it's okay to let go. This section helps you recognize when it's time to move on and what to do next.

☠️ Knowing When a Relationship Is Toxic

A toxic relationship isn't just one that has fights. It's one that constantly makes you doubt your worth or feel unsafe. Signs include:

- They put you down, even as a joke
- You feel anxious after talking to them
- They ignore your boundaries
- You feel like you can't be yourself
- You're always the one apologizing

If this feels familiar, trust your gut. A healthy relationship should make you feel respected and safe, not confused or small. You don't need a big reason to leave. Feeling worn out is reason enough. You deserve connections that nourish, not drain.

SOS Who to Talk to for Support

Leaving any relationship can feel lonely. But you don't have to go through it alone. I found so much comfort in talking to someone I trusted. Here's who you might turn to:

- A close friend who listens without judging
- A teacher, counselor, or coach
- A sibling or adult who cares about your well-being
- A therapist who can guide you through your feelings

Sometimes it helps just to hear, "You're not crazy for feeling this way." Support gives you the strength to make hard choices. Don't keep it bottled up. Sharing helps you feel seen and reminds you that you're not alone in this.

Did You Know?

Your brain is wired for connection, which is why ending a relationship can feel so painful even if it's the right choice. Studies show that emotional pain from rejection or break-ups activates the same parts of the brain as physical pain. That's why it can feel like something's physically breaking inside you.

That's why walking away can hurt, even when you're protecting your peace. But here's the good news: research also shows that setting boundaries and ending unhealthy relationships leads to better mental health, stronger self-esteem, and a clearer sense of identity over time. The relief may not come right away, but it does come.

Letting go isn't giving up. It's an act of self-care. You're not weak for feeling sad. You're strong for choosing what's best for your well-being. Strength sometimes looks like quiet, brave decisions no one else sees.

📄 Break-Up Boundary Plan

Whether it's a romantic break-up or a friend break-up, setting boundaries after the end matters. You don't owe constant contact or explanations. You get to choose what feels right for your healing.

Make a plan:

- Will you unfollow or mute them on social media?
- Do you want space or a clean break from contact?
- What will you say if they reach out again?
- Who can you text instead when you feel low?

Having a plan makes the hard moments a little easier. You're allowed to protect your peace. Boundaries after a break-up aren't mean. They're self-respect.

🌱 Self-Care After a Friendship Ends

Losing a close friendship hurts. Even when it's the right choice, there's grief. I've cried over friendships more than I have over relationships. Give yourself space to feel.

Self-care ideas:

- Write in your journal to release feelings
- Move your body or go for a long walk
- Listen to music that soothes or uplifts you
- Remind yourself of what you learned from the experience
- Reconnect with people who truly care about you

Healing doesn't mean forgetting. It means forgiving yourself, finding meaning, and growing stronger. You're not broken because someone walked away or because you did. You're just becoming more you.

📖 Story Time: The Time I Said No and Didn't Regret It

There was a time when a close friend kept calling me late at night to vent. At first, I wanted to be there, but after a while, it started to drain me. I'd lie awake for hours afterward, anxious and unable to sleep. Still, I felt guilty even thinking about saying anything. What kind of friend says "no" to someone who's hurting?

One night, I finally texted, "I care about you, but I need to take care of my own mental health too. Can we talk earlier in the day instead?" I was nervous they'd be mad. But they actually said, "I get it. Thanks for being honest."

That moment changed everything for me. It reminded me that setting a boundary doesn't mean pushing people away. It means choosing honesty and care for them and for yourself.

Chapter Wrap-Up

Self-esteem doesn't grow from perfection or pretending everything's fine. It grows from how you respond to yourself, especially when things are hard. This chapter helped you do just that. You met your inner critic, gave it a name, and started to recognize when it shows up. More importantly, you began learning how to talk back, not with more shame, but with honesty and self-respect.

You practiced treating yourself like a friend, rewriting old patterns of harsh thoughts, and using tools like positive self-talk and identity maps to build a steadier view of who you are. You stopped letting your appearance define your worth and started seeing your strengths in how you think, care, and show up. You learned to celebrate real wins like tiny ones, brave ones, and the ones no one sees. Confidence wasn't something you had to wait for.

This chapter reminded you that how you speak to yourself matters. And you're learning to speak with courage, not cruelty. That's a strength. That's growth. And it's already inside you.

Now that you've got the people side down, let's focus on you. Chapter 8 is all about crushing goals, building habits, and actually following through.

🏠 Parents' Corner: Let's Think Together

Activity: What Does Respect Sound Like?

Spend 20 to 30 minutes together talking about communication styles in your home. Try this simple activity:

- Everyone shares one thing that makes them feel respected in a conversation
- Then, everyone shares one thing that makes it hard to speak up
- Keep it judgment-free. The goal is not to fix or defend. It is to understand and grow.

Support Your Teen By:

- Pausing before reacting to emotional moments
- Modeling how to say "no" with kindness, not guilt
- Owning your mistakes and repairing them out loud
- Letting them express needs, even when they are different from yours

Let your teen see that healthy communication is something you are working on, too. It builds trust, not just skills.

You are not just raising someone who knows how to speak. You are showing them how to be heard and still stay kind.

🔑 Key Takeaways

- Your inner critic is not the truth. It is a habit of thought shaped by past voices, not your present reality.
- Talking to yourself like a friend builds self-respect and quiets shame-based thinking.
- You are more than your looks. Strength, kindness, curiosity, and courage are all part of your worth.

- Noticing your wins, no matter how small, helps retrain your brain to see progress instead of failure.
- Confidence grows through practice. Trying new things, using your body language, and affirming your efforts help you build it from the inside out.

Exercise 1: Worry Box

Write your worries on slips of paper and place them in a box. Open the box once a week to check if they came true. Use the space below to record some of them.

My Worries:

Weekly Reflection (Did they come true? How do I feel now?):

Exercise 2: What's the Worst That Could Happen?

Write your worry. Then list the worst case, best case, and most likely scenario.

My Worry:

Worst Case Scenario:

Best Case Scenario:

Most Likely Scenario:

Reflection (How does this change how I see the worry?):

CHAPTER 8:

Goal Getters - Motivation, Habits, and Follow-Through

"You don't have to see the whole staircase, just take the first step.

— Martin Luther King Jr.

WHEN I FIRST started setting goals, I often felt like I had to figure everything out at once. I looked at the big dream; it seemed so far away that I did not know where to begin. Maybe you have felt the same way. You want to do something important, but the distance between where you are and where you want to be feels overwhelming. The good news is you do not need to have it all mapped out today. What matters is that you start. In this chapter, I will walk with you through the process of turning big dreams into small steps, creating habits that stick, finding motivation through action, and learning how to bounce back when things do not go as planned. Together, we will focus on progress and celebrate every win along the way.

Dream Big (Then Break It Down)

I used to think big dreams were only for people who had everything figured out. The truth is, dreaming big is for everyone, including you. This section explores how to create a vision, set goals you can measure, and map out the steps that will take you from where you are to where you want to be.

Vision Board Activity

When you can see your dream in front of you, it feels more real. A vision board is a tool that helps you create that picture and keep it close to you. It reminds you of your "why" every single day, even when you feel tired or distracted.

A vision board works best when you:

- Collect images, drawings, or words that inspire you
- Use a poster, notebook, or digital board on your phone
- Place it where you'll see it daily for motivation
- Refresh or update it as your dreams grow

Looking at your vision board is like sending your brain a message that your dream matters. It's not just about pretty pictures; it's about focus. The more often you see your goals, the more natural it feels to work toward them. A vision board turns "someday" into a daily reminder of possibility.

🎯 Turning Dreams into SMART Goals

Big dreams often stay dreams because they aren't clear enough. That's why SMART goals are so helpful. They take something huge and vague and turn it into a plan you can actually follow. SMART stands for Specific, Measurable, Achievable, Relevant, and Time-bound. When you apply this to your dream, you create a roadmap.

Here's how to use SMART goals:

- **Specific:** Define exactly what you want
- **Measurable:** Decide how you'll track progress
- **Achievable:** Choose something realistic for your life now
- **Relevant:** Pick a goal that matters to you personally
- **Time-bound:** Set a clear deadline to keep momentum

For example, instead of saying, "I want to be healthier," you could say, "I will walk for 20 minutes after school, three days a week, for the next month." SMART goals keep you focused and remind you that progress is possible. You no longer just wish; you take action.

Goal Ladder: Steps from Here to There

Climbing toward a dream is like climbing a ladder. You can't leap to the top in one move, but you can take it step by step. A goal ladder helps you see that progress builds over time. It shows you that every small step counts and brings you closer to your dream.

Here's how to build your ladder:

- Write your big dream at the very top
- List the smaller steps needed to reach it
- Organize the steps in order, from easiest to hardest
- Check off each step when you complete it

For example, if your dream is to play guitar at a concert, your ladder might include learning chords, playing a full song, practicing for family, and finally performing on stage. Each rung is progress. The ladder proves that success is not about giant leaps but about steady effort. Climbing slowly builds strength, confidence, and momentum.

🧠 Did You Know?

Your brain actually loves clear goals. When you set a specific and measurable target, your brain releases dopamine, the "reward chemical." That's why checking off even a small step feels so good; it's your brain encouraging you to keep going. Vague goals like "be better at math" don't spark the same response. But saying, "I'll practice ten problems a day," lights up your brain's motivation system.

🤔 The Motivation Myth

I used to believe that I had to "feel motivated" before I could get anything done. The truth is, motivation rarely shows up on its own. If you wait until you feel like it, you'll probably be waiting a long time. This section explores why waiting for motivation doesn't work, how action sparks drive, and how you can use simple tools to stay on track even when you don't feel like it.

Motivation comes and goes; habits and discipline are what keep you on track.

⏳ Why Waiting to "Feel Motivated" Doesn't Work

Motivation is not a magic spark that suddenly appears. If you wait until you feel ready, you might never start. I've learned that motivation usually shows up after you've already taken action, not before. The idea that you'll feel perfectly prepared is a myth. Here's why waiting doesn't work:

- Feelings come and go, and they aren't reliable for planning
- If you wait, fear or doubt often grows stronger
- Starting small builds more energy than waiting for the "perfect time"
- Motivation is a side effect of progress, not the starting point

When you stop waiting for the "right mood," you permit yourself to begin imperfectly. Action, even tiny action, builds momentum. The first step is the hardest, but once you take it, the rest feels easier.

💥 Action Leads to Motivation, Not the Other Way

I used to think I needed motivation before I could act, but it turns out the opposite is true. When you take action, no matter how small, it sparks energy that makes you want to keep going. Think of it like pushing a heavy door: once it starts to move, it becomes easier to keep pushing.

Here's how action builds motivation:

- Doing one small thing signals to your brain that progress is happening
- Each completed step creates a sense of reward and pride
- Your energy grows when you see results, even small ones
- Momentum makes the next step feel less overwhelming

The trick is to start with the smallest action possible. That first step sends a message to your brain: "I'm moving forward." Motivation follows behind. You don't need to feel ready to begin; you need to begin to feel ready.

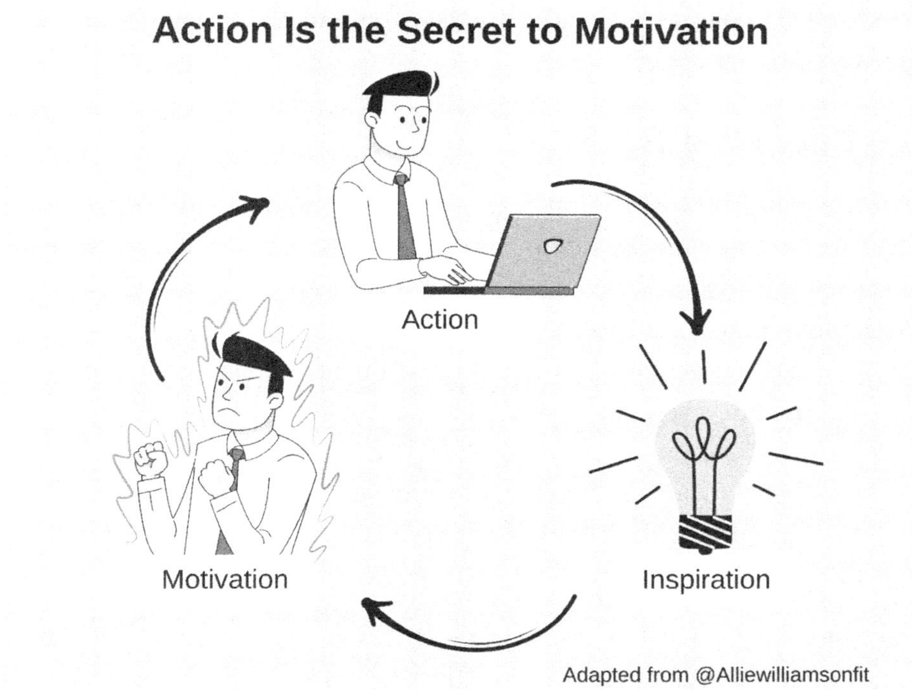

Make a Motivation Menu

There will be days when you feel stuck, and that's when a motivation menu can help. A motivation menu is a list of simple actions that give you a boost. Instead of waiting to feel inspired, you choose something from the menu and do it. Your menu might include:

- Listening to a short upbeat song
- Writing a quick to-do list with only one or two tasks
- Doing a five-minute stretch or walk
- Talking to a supportive friend or family member
- Reviewing your vision board or a quote that inspires you

The point of a motivation menu is to give you quick options that spark energy. You don't have to rely on willpower alone. When you feel stuck, pick one item and try it. Small sparks can restart your engine and get you moving again.

Daily Wins Tracker

Motivation grows when you notice your progress. A daily wins tracker is a simple way to record small victories, no matter how tiny they seem. I started writing mine in a notebook, but you can also use your phone or a calendar. Here's how to use one:

- Write down one to three things you accomplished each day
- Include even small wins, like "I finished my homework" or "I asked for help"
- Review your list at the end of the week to see your progress
- Celebrate effort, not just big results

Tracking wins trains your brain to see progress instead of only focusing on what's left undone. With time, you'll start to feel more confident because you have proof that you are moving forward. A daily wins tracker shifts your focus from pressure to progress, and that's where real motivation grows.

Fun Fact

Research shows that simply starting a task, even for just two minutes, can flip your brain into "focus mode." Psychologists call this the "Zeigarnik effect," which means your mind doesn't like leaving things unfinished. That's why washing one dish often leads to cleaning the whole sink, or writing one sentence can turn into finishing your homework. Action pulls motivation behind it.

Make It a Habit

I used to think habits were only about discipline or willpower, but they are really about patterns your brain learns to repeat. The good news is that you can design those patterns to work for you instead of against you. This section explores how habits are formed, why small changes matter, and how tools like trackers and stacking can help you build routines that stick.

🔄 The Habit Loop: Cue, Routine, Reward

Every habit follows a loop: a cue triggers it, the routine is the action, and the reward is what keeps it going. Once you notice this pattern, you can start to shape it. Here's how it works:

- Cue: Something that starts the habit (like an alarm or seeing your shoes)
- Routine: The action you take (like brushing your teeth or going for a jog)
- Reward: The benefit your brain gets (like a clean feeling or a burst of energy)
- The brain repeats habits because it expects the reward

For example, if your cue is your phone alarm at 7:00 pm, your routine might be ten minutes of studying, and your reward could be a fun break afterward. Understanding the loop gives you the power to build habits that serve your goals instead of letting bad habits run the show.

🌱 Tiny Habits That Make a Big Difference

Big changes often start with the tiniest actions. I used to think I had to do everything at once, but I learned that small habits create momentum. Tiny habits may not seem important at first, but when you repeat them daily, they add up to something huge. Some powerful tiny habits are:

- Drinking one glass of water first thing in the morning
- Writing down one thing you're grateful for each night
- Taking five deep breaths when you feel stressed
- Reading two pages of a book each day
- Lying out your clothes the night before

The goal is not perfection. The goal is consistency. With time, tiny habits build confidence and progress. They are easier to start and easier to stick with, and they train your brain to believe, "I can do this."

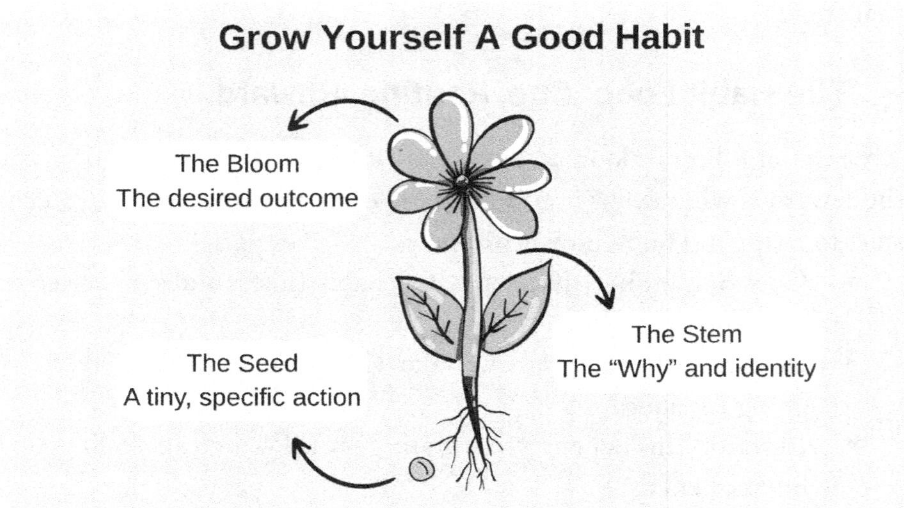

📊 Habit Tracker Template

A habit tracker is a visual way to remind yourself of progress. It shows you what you've done and helps you stay consistent. Seeing your progress on paper or on a screen can motivate you to keep going, even on tough days. Here's how to use a tracker:

- Choose one or two habits you want to build
- Create a simple grid in a notebook, calendar, or app
- Mark each day you complete the habit with a check, color, or symbol
- Review your tracker weekly to notice patterns

For example, if you want to journal three times a week, you can check off each day you write. The more boxes you fill, the more momentum you feel. A tracker is like proof that your effort matters. The act of checking off a day becomes its own reward, reminding you that progress is happening.

Habit Stacking Practice

Habit stacking means connecting a new habit to one you already do. This makes it easier to remember and harder to skip because the habit fits into something familiar. I've found this technique powerful because it removes the need for constant reminders.

Here's how to stack habits:

- Identify a habit you already do daily (like brushing your teeth or making tea)
- Add a small new habit right after it
- Keep the new habit simple and short
- Repeat until it feels automatic

For example, "After I brush my teeth, I will floss one tooth," or "After I pour my morning tea, I will write one sentence in my journal." Stacking works because your brain links the new habit to something automatic. With time, the new behavior sticks, and you expand it naturally. It's like building a chain of habits that support the life you want.

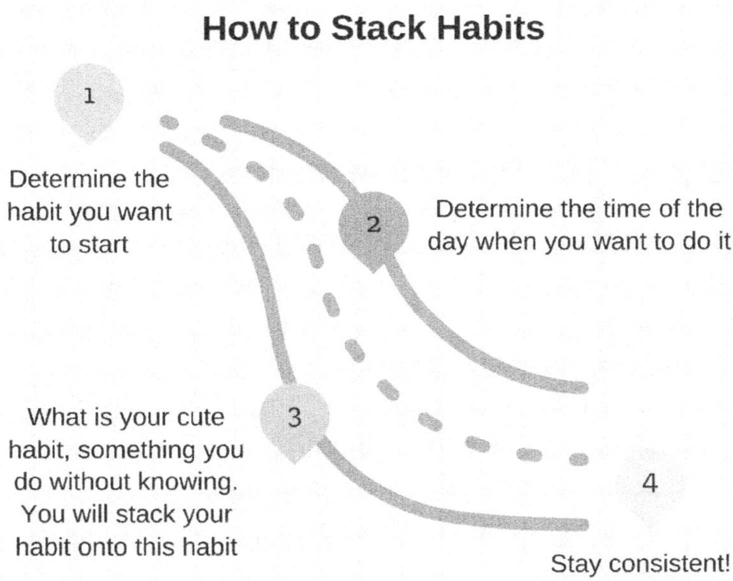

Adapted from lifebydeanna.com

🌪️ The Bump	💡 Big Idea	🚀 Your Move
Setbacks Happen	Mistakes don't erase progress.	Focus on the next step.
What's Next Matters	Progress is not perfection.	Learn, don't quit.
Self-Forgiveness	Kindness speeds recovery.	Say: "I can try again."
Reset Plans	Backups keep momentum.	Plan B: small step Plan C: bare minimum
Comeback Story	You're the hero rising again.	Draw your challenge and recovery.

🎉 Celebrate Progress

When I first started working on my goals, I often skipped celebrating because I felt I wasn't "there yet." But I've learned that progress, not perfection, is what truly builds confidence. Celebrating small wins fuels motivation and reminds you how far you've come. This section explores why progress deserves recognition, how to reflect weekly, and creative ways to celebrate your wins with yourself and others.

❇️ Progress, Not Perfection Mantra

Chasing perfection only leads to frustration. The truth is, progress, no matter how small, means you are moving forward. Keep this mantra in mind:

- "Progress is proof I'm growing."
- "Small wins are still wins."
- "I don't need perfect to be proud."
- "Every step counts, even the messy ones."

Repeat this mantra when you feel stuck. It shifts your focus from what you have not done to what you are doing. By celebrating progress, you stay motivated even when things are not flawless.

Celebrate every single win, no matter it's size.

Weekly Reflection Prompts

Reflection is like checking your map during a journey. It helps you see where you have been and what direction you are going. Taking a few minutes each week to reflect keeps you aware of your progress.

Try these prompts:

- What's one win I had this week?
- What challenge did I face, and how did I handle it?
- What habit did I stick with?
- What can I try differently next week?

Write your answers in a journal or notes app. Reflection helps you see that even small efforts matter. You will notice patterns, learn from mistakes, and find encouragement to keep going. Weekly reflection is not about judgment. It is about learning and celebrating.

🧱 Make a Victory Wall

A victory wall is a fun and visual way to celebrate your achievements. It is like keeping a highlight reel of your progress where you can see it every day. Here's how to make one:

- Choose a wall, corkboard, or poster
- Add sticky notes for each win, no matter how small
- Use drawings, photos, or quotes that remind you of your growth
- Update it regularly with new victories

With time, your wall becomes a collection of proof that you are moving forward. On tough days, looking at your victory wall reminds you of how much you have already accomplished. It is a powerful way to keep your motivation alive.

🥂 Share a Win With Someone You Trust

Celebrating progress does not have to be a solo act. Sharing your wins with someone supportive makes the victory feel even stronger. It also builds connection and accountability. Here's how to share:

- Tell a friend, parent, or mentor about a recent success
- Be honest, even if the win feels small
- Notice how they respond with encouragement
- Let their support fuel your next step

When you share your wins, you allow others to celebrate you, too. It creates a positive cycle of encouragement, and you might even inspire them to share their wins with you. Celebrating together strengthens relationships and reminds you that growth is worth honoring.

📖 Story Time: My Victory Wall Surprise

When I first started tracking wins, I felt silly writing down things like, "I studied for 15 minutes" or "I went for a walk." They seemed too small to matter. But after a few weeks, I looked at the notes I had pinned on my wall, and it shocked me. The tiny steps had added up. I saw the effort I had ignored before. On a day when I felt discouraged, I read through those notes and realized, "I am not failing, I am growing." That moment stayed with me. It showed me that progress hides in plain sight unless you pause to notice it. Celebrating each step does not make you arrogant; it makes you aware of your strength.

📌 Chapter Wrap-Up

Motivation is not something you wait for; it grows when you take action. This chapter showed you how to break down big dreams into smaller steps and turn them into SMART goals. You learned to climb one rung at a time with goal ladders, spark energy through action, and track wins to build confidence. Habits, not willpower, create lasting progress, and setbacks become opportunities to reset. Progress, not perfection, is the real measure of growth.

With your motivation engine running, it's time to tackle fear head-on, Chapter 9 is where we become worry warriors and take control of anxiety.

🏠 Parents' Corner: Let's Think Together

Activity: What's One Step You Took Today?

Spend 15 to 20 minutes together talking about progress. Try this simple activity:

- Everyone shares one small win they had today, no matter how tiny.
- Then, everyone shares one step they want to try tomorrow.

Keep it light and supportive. The goal is not to measure who did more, but to notice that every step forward matters.

Support Your Teen By:

- Modeling how to turn big dreams into small actions
- Sharing your own reset plan when you miss a goal
- Celebrating effort, not just results
- Helping them track wins visually, like on a calendar or wall chart
- Showing that success is about progress, not perfection

When you practice goal-setting as a family, you are not just teaching responsibility. You are showing your teen that steady steps build confidence and growth.

Key Takeaways

- Big dreams become reachable when broken into smaller steps.
- SMART goals (Specific, Measurable, Achievable, Relevant, Time-bound) turn vague wishes into action plans.
- Action creates motivation; waiting for the "perfect time" only delays progress.
- Habits grow from cues, routines, and rewards, and even tiny changes add up.
- Setbacks do not erase effort; reset plans and self-forgiveness keep you on track.
- Celebrating small wins builds confidence and reminds you that you are moving forward.

Exercise 1: Dream Board

Create a vision board with images and words that show what you want to achieve. You can cut out pictures, draw, or write them here.

My Dream Board Ideas:

____

____

____

(Attach or draw pictures here)

Exercise 2: SMART Goal Builder

Choose one goal and turn it into a SMART goal: Specific, Measurable, Achievable, Relevant, and Time-bound.

My Goal:

____

Specific:

____

Measurable:

____

Achievable:

____

Relevant:

____

Time-Bound:

____

My Final SMART Goal Statement:

____

CHAPTER 9:

Worry Warriors - CBT for Tackling Anxiety and Fear

"Fear is only as deep as the mind allows."

— Japanese Proverb

ANXIETY CAN FEEL like it defines who you are, but it is only one part of your experience. I used to think worry meant I was weak or broken, but I've learned that it is simply your brain's way of trying to keep you safe. The problem is, it often goes overboard and leaves you feeling stuck, shaky, or overwhelmed. You do not have to let fear control your choices or your life. This chapter explores how to understand your worry, face it with practical tools, and build confidence by taking small steps toward calm. You will meet your "worry monster," learn quick body hacks for anxious moments, and create your own calm kit to carry with you.

Meet Your Inner Worry Monster

Anxiety can feel like an invisible weight that follows you around, but giving it a shape can help you understand it better. Instead of ignoring your worries, try to picture them as a "Worry Monster." When you name it, describe it, and see how it shows up in your body, it becomes easier to face. This section explores what anxiety feels like, how to draw or describe your Worry Monster, what it tells you, and why it actually thinks it's helping.

🎨 Draw or Describe Your Worry Monster

Sometimes it helps to make your anxiety visual. Giving it a silly or strange appearance can make it feel less powerful. Instead of letting the fear stay hidden, you drag it into the light where you can see it clearly. Once you can see it, it is easier to laugh at and talk back to.

Try this:

- Draw your Worry Monster in your journal
- Describe its size, color, or voice
- Give it a funny name like "Naggy Nelly" or "Buzz Brain"
- Add speech bubbles of what it usually says

When you see your worry on paper, it feels less like a shadow and more like something you can respond to. It gives you a chance to be creative and playful with something that used to feel heavy. With time, you may even start to notice your monster losing its power.

What It Says vs. What's True

Your Worry Monster often lies. It tries to protect you but ends up scaring you instead. The trick is learning to catch the lies quickly and replace them with something more helpful. The more often you do this, the more natural it feels to push back against worry. Here's how to catch it:

- **Worry Monster:** "You'll mess up." **Truth:** "Everyone makes mistakes, but I can handle it."
- **Worry Monster:** "Something bad will happen." **Truth:** "I don't know the future, but I can deal with challenges."
- **Worry Monster:** "You can't do this." **Truth:** "I've done hard things before. I can do this too."

Replacing its voice with the truth takes away its power. At first, it might feel like you're pretending, but with practice, your brain starts to believe the truth instead of the fear. Soon you'll notice the monster getting quieter each time you stand up to it.

Why It Thinks It's Helping

The Worry Monster is not your enemy. It's just confused. In a strange way, it believes it is doing you a favor by keeping you cautious. But just because it means well does not mean it knows best. Think of it like this:

- It wants to keep you safe
- It warns you of possible danger
- It overreacts, even when there's no real threat
- It believes stress will prepare you

Remind yourself that the Worry Monster is trying to help but doesn't always get it right. You can thank it for caring and then choose what to believe. This helps you feel in control instead of trapped by fear. In time, you'll see the monster more as a nervous helper than a scary boss.

From Panic to Plan

Panic can feel like a sudden storm that sweeps you away. Your chest tightens, your mind races, and you feel powerless. But panic does not have to control you. With a plan, you can steady yourself and move through it. This section explores how to make a coping card, what helps you in anxious moments, how to practice being a friend to yourself, and how to use the circle of control activity.

Create a Coping Card

A coping card is a small but powerful tool. In anxious moments, it is hard to remember what helps. Writing calming steps on a card gives you something to hold onto when your mind feels scrambled. Here's what to put on it:

- Three calming strategies, like deep breathing, grounding, or stretching
- A reminder, such as "This will pass."
- Names of people you can text or call
- One healthy action, like listening to music or drawing

Keep the card in your wallet, bag, or phone case. When panic rises, you do not have to figure it out in the moment. You already have a guide waiting for you, and that makes you feel ready.

🛠 What Helps You in Anxious Moments?

Every person finds comfort in different ways. What eases one person's nerves may not work for someone else. Discovering what works for you gives you confidence in anxious moments. Ideas to try:

- Breathe in for four counts and out for six
- Hold something cold, like an ice cube
- Play a song that lifts your mood
- Move your body with walking, stretching, or jumping jacks

Notice which activities calm you the fastest and write them down. A personal list of tools means you always know where to turn. Instead of guessing, you have trusted strategies that make panic less overwhelming.

💬 Rehearse: What Would You Say to a Friend?

Anxiety often makes you talk to yourself harshly or fearfully. Yet if your best friend were panicking, you would encourage them with kindness. Practicing that same care with yourself is a powerful skill. Try this:

- Imagine your best friend is anxious
- Write down what you would say, such as "You are safe, breathe, I am here."
- Practice saying those same words to yourself
- Repeat them until they feel familiar and natural

Speaking gently to yourself creates a calming inner voice. You begin to replace fear with support, just as you would for someone you love. That voice becomes a steady reminder that you can get through the moment.

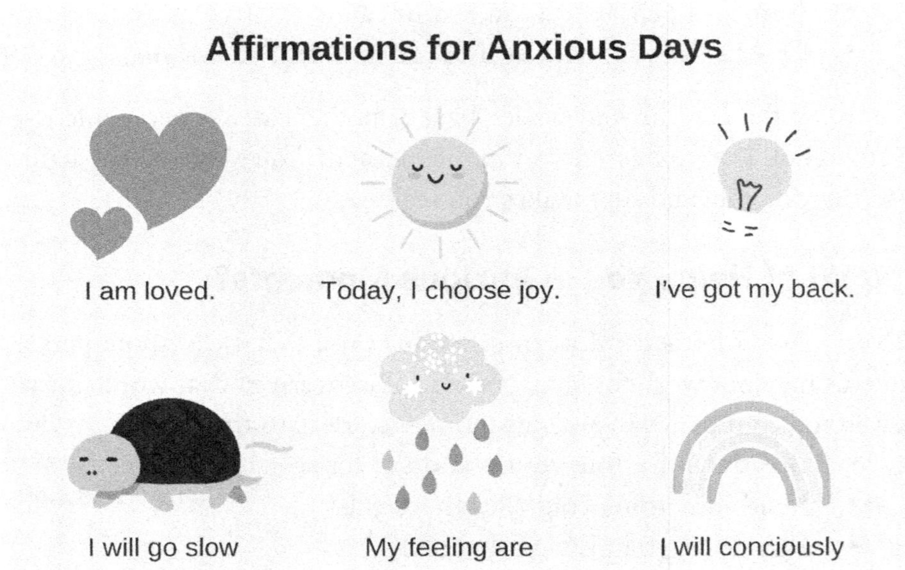

Circle of Control Activity

Anxiety can make you worry about things far outside your control. The circle of control activity helps you separate what is truly yours to manage from what is not. Here's how to do it:

- Draw two circles, one inside the other
- In the smaller circle, write what you can control (your choices, your actions, your effort)
- In the outer circle, write what you cannot control (the past, other people's opinions, the weather)
- When panic comes, focus on the smaller circle

This practice helps you put your energy where it matters. You feel lighter because you stop trying to carry what is not in your hands. By focusing on your circle, you regain a sense of calm and direction.

Everything Out of Control, Also Out of Mind

Body Hacks for Anxiety

Anxiety is not only in your thoughts. It also shows up in your body with racing heartbeats, shaky hands, or tight muscles. I know how overwhelming it feels when your body reacts before your mind can even catch up. This section explores fast breathing techniques, progressive muscle relaxation, simple hacks like cold water or movement, and a way to track how much these tools help.

Breathing Techniques That Work Fast

Breathing is one of the quickest ways to calm your nervous system. When anxiety hits, your breath often becomes short and shallow, which tells your body to stay on high alert. Shifting your breathing pattern tells your brain that it is safe to relax. Try these options:

- **Box breathing:** Inhale 4, hold 4, exhale 4, hold 4
- **4-6 breathing:** Inhale for 4, exhale for 6
- **Belly breathing:** Place a hand on your stomach and breathe deeply so your hand rises

Practice these when you are calm so they are easier to use in tough moments. The more you practice, the more automatic it becomes. Breathing techniques give you an anchor and remind you that you have power even when anxiety feels big.

Shrink the Scary Stuff

Fear makes challenges feel bigger than they are, but steady steps shrink it. Try these tools to build calm and courage:

- **Exposure Ladder:** Face fears step by step, starting small and moving up only when ready. Each step proves you can handle more.
- **Fear vs. Danger:** Ask, Am I safe right now? Most fear is "what if," not real threat. Naming the difference brings clarity.
- **Best-Case Thinking:** Instead of worst-case, picture what could go right. Visualizing success rewires your brain toward hope.
- **Pep Talk Journal:** Write kind reminders like "I can handle this." Read them when anxiety speaks loudest.

Small practices, repeated often, make fear lose its power.

Progressive Muscle Relaxation

Tension often builds in your muscles during anxious moments. Progressive muscle relaxation helps release that tightness by tensing and relaxing muscles in a step-by-step way. It brings awareness to your body and creates a sense of release. Here is one way to do it:

- Sit or lie down in a quiet place
- Start at your feet and curl your toes tightly for 5 seconds
- Release and notice the difference
- Move upward through your legs, stomach, hands, shoulders, and face

- Finish with a few slow breaths

This practice teaches you the difference between tension and relaxation. By cycling through your muscles, you give your body permission to let go of stress. The more you practice, the easier it becomes to notice tension early and relax before it builds too much.

Cold Water Splash or Movement Hacks

Quick physical changes can jolt your system out of panic. Cold water or sudden movement signals to your brain that the situation is shifting, which helps lower the intensity of anxious feelings. Here are a few hacks:

- Splash cold water on your face
- Hold an ice cube in your hand until it melts
- Do 20 jumping jacks or march in place
- Shake out your arms and legs like you are releasing energy

These actions distract your mind while calming your body's alarm system. They may sound simple, but they often provide instant relief. Having a few of these hacks ready means you always have a way to shift your state when anxiety feels overwhelming.

📊 Rate Your Anxiety Before and After Each Tool

Tracking your anxiety levels helps you see the real impact of body hacks. This turns calming exercises into measurable progress, which builds your confidence in using them. Here's how:

- Before trying a tool, rate your anxiety from 1 to 10
- Use one of the strategies, such as breathing, muscle relaxation, or movement
- Rate your anxiety again afterward
- Write down the changes in a journal or notes app

Even if your number drops only a little, it is proof that the tool worked. With time, you will see patterns and discover which strategies help you most. Recording your progress reminds you that you are capable of calming yourself and that anxiety is not in full control.

Did You Know?

Slow breathing works because it tells your vagus nerve, a nerve that runs from your brain to your body, that it is safe to relax. When the vagus nerve is activated, it lowers your heart rate and eases muscle tension. It's like pressing your body's natural "calm button."

Create Your Calm Kit

When anxiety shows up, it helps to have tools ready instead of scrambling for comfort. I have learned that a calm kit gives me choices when my mind feels stuck. You can create your own collection of people, places, and activities that bring you peace. This section explores how to build your calm kit, what to keep in it, and how to use it when stress feels overwhelming.

📄 List of Go-To Calmers

Think about what makes you feel safe and steady. These are your go-to calmers. Everyone's list looks different, and that's what makes it personal. What calms you may not calm someone else, so focus on what feels good for you. Some examples include:

- a Talking to a trusted person
- Listening to a calming playlist
- Spending time in a cozy or quiet space
- Hugging pet or using a soft blanket

Write down your personal list and keep it handy. The more options you have, the more prepared you'll feel. Having go-to calmers makes it easier to soothe yourself before anxiety takes over.

🎶 Pack a Mini Calm Kit for Your Backpack

A calm kit doesn't need to be big. A small version you can carry daily is just as powerful. By keeping it simple, you make sure it's something you'll actually use instead of leaving it at home. Even tiny comforts can make a big difference when you're overwhelmed.

Try including:

- Stress ball or fidget toy
- Headphones for calming music
- A small notebook or doodle pad
- A favorite scent, like lavender lotion

This kit can travel with you anywhere, ready when you need it most. You don't have to use everything at once. Even one item can ground you in a tough moment. Carrying a calm kit is like carrying a safety net, reminding you that you're not powerless against stress.

✉ Write a Note to Your Future Anxious Self

When you're calm, write a note to the version of you who feels anxious. This note works like a reminder that you have been through hard moments before and found your way through. Sometimes, hearing encouragement from your own voice is the most believable support you can receive. Ideas for your note:

- Remind yourself that the feeling will pass
- Write down things that have helped before
- Encourage yourself with kind words
- Remind yourself of your strengths

Tuck this note into your calm kit. When anxiety rises, read it and hear your own supportive voice. It can be surprisingly powerful to receive encouragement from yourself. A kind note is proof that even in hard moments, you have your own back.

🔍 Check-In: What Helped Most This Week?

Your calm kit will work best when you update it. At the end of each week, check in with yourself. These check-ins are not about judgment but about noticing what's working. With time, this practice teaches you to trust your own ability to adjust and grow.

Ask:

- Which calmer helped me most?
- Did I try something new that worked?
- Is there something I want to add or remove?
- What pattern do I notice about my stress?

This check-in helps you shape a kit that truly fits you. It also reminds you that you're making progress. A calm kit is not just a box of tools. It is a reflection of how you learn, adapt, and grow stronger in managing anxiety.

Story Time: My Worry Monster at Night

When I was younger, I often lay awake at night with my mind racing. Every creak in the house became proof that something bad was about to happen. My "Worry Monster" whispered, "You are not safe," and I believed it. One night, I decided to draw what it looked like. I gave it a funny face, floppy ears, and a squeaky voice. Suddenly, it seemed less powerful. Looking at my silly drawing made me laugh, and in that moment, I realized I could shrink my fear by changing how I saw it. That was the first time I felt in charge of my worry instead of the other way around.

Rising Through Hard Times: Building Real Resilience

Life will test you in ways you never expect. Some days feel unfair, some moments too heavy to carry, and yet within those struggles lies the chance to grow stronger. Resilience is not about avoiding pain or pretending you are unshaken—it is about finding the courage to face storms, cope with loss, lean on others, and discover the strength you did not know you had. This section brings together the tools, reflections, and truths that help you rise again, no matter how many times you fall.

Facing Life's Storms

Life will not always be fair, and sometimes the storms that come your way are beyond your control. You may feel powerless, but you always have a choice in how you respond. Expressing your struggles—whether by drawing your storm, writing in a journal, or naming your feelings—helps you take what feels overwhelming inside and put it into a form you can face.

Coping With Stress

Stress is unavoidable, but you can prepare for it. A survival kit filled with comforting tools, a personal stress scale to track how overwhelmed you feel, and steady self-talk all make the storm less consuming. Reminding yourself, "This is temporary" or "I can take one step at a time" creates calm where panic might otherwise grow.

Leaning on Support

Hard times feel heavier when you think you are alone. Creating a map of your support network or writing down your "team" reminds you who you can lean on. Asking for help is not a weakness—it is a sign of courage and trust. Friends, family, teachers, mentors, or therapists can all play a role in lifting the weight when it feels too much.

🕯️ Living With Loss

Grief comes in many forms, from losing people to saying goodbye to friendships, places, or dreams. Naming your loss, building a memory box, or writing a goodbye letter allows you to honor what mattered without holding it all inside. Healing is not a straight line, and mixed emotions—sadness, laughter, anger, even guilt—are all part of the process.

Finding Strength in Reflection

Every struggle leaves behind a mark of strength. Reflecting on challenges you have already lived through shows you patience, courage, and persistence you may not have seen before. Writing your survivor story or leaving a letter for your future self turns pain into proof that you can keep rising, even when life knocks you down.

❤️ The Heart of Resilience

Resilience is not about avoiding hardship or pretending you are unshaken. It is about facing storms with honesty, choosing small steps forward, leaning on support, honoring your grief, and remembering your own strength. Each time you rise again, you are not the same as before—you are stronger, wiser, and more prepared for the road ahead.

📌 Chapter Wrap-Up

Anxiety is not a weakness; it is your brain trying too hard to protect you. In this chapter, you gave your Worry Monster a face and a name, and you practiced noticing what it says versus what is true. You built coping tools like cards, calm kits, and body hacks to steady yourself in anxious moments. You learned that fear shrinks when faced in small steps, and that progress grows through practice.

In this chapter, you've learned to manage thoughts, feelings, and fears. Now it's time to explore who you really are and how to fully belong in the world. Do your exercises and let's move on to the final chapter.

🏠 Parents' Corner: Let's Think Together

Activity: What Calms You Fastest?

Spend 15 minutes together trying calming strategies. Each person shares one tool that helps when they feel anxious, like deep breathing, stretching, or music. Then, let each family member try someone else's idea. Notice which ones help most.

Support Your Teen By:

- Naming your own stress signals out loud
- Practicing body hacks like breathing or movement with them
- Keeping a family calm kit in a shared space
- Talking about times you faced worry and got through it
- Reminding them that fear shrinks when faced slowly

Showing your teen that you practice these tools too builds trust and reminds them they are not alone in learning to manage fear.

🔑 Key Takeaways

- Anxiety is a safety system that sometimes overreacts.
- Naming your Worry Monster makes it easier to face.
- Coping cards, calm kits, and body hacks help in stressful moments.
- Exposure ladders shrink fear step by step.
- Best-case thinking and pep talk journaling balance negative thoughts.
- Progress, not perfection, is what weakens anxiety over time.them they are not alone in learning to manage fear.

Exercise 1: One-Minute Focus

Set a timer for 1 minute. Focus only on your breath or an object. Afterward, write how it felt.

What I Focused On (breath/object):

____

How It Felt:

____

____

____

____

____

____

Exercise 2: Nature Noticing

Go outside and list five things you've never noticed before.

1. ______________________________
2. ______________________________
3. ______________________________
4. ______________________________

____

Reflection (How paying attention changed my experience):

____

____

____

____

____

____

🙋 CHAPTER 10:

Identity & Belonging - Be You, for Real

"To be yourself in a world that is constantly trying to make you something else is the greatest accomplishment."

— Ralph Waldo Emerson

WHEN I WAS younger, I often struggled with the question, Who am I really? I tried to fit into groups, wear the right clothes, or act in ways I thought would make others accept me. Maybe you have felt that pressure too. It can feel exhausting to keep changing yourself just to belong, only to end up feeling more lost inside. I learned that true belonging is not about fitting in. It is about showing up as your real self and finding the people who welcome you as you are. You do not need to have every answer right now. Identity is something you explore and grow into, piece by piece. In this chapter, I will walk with you through discovering your identity, finding supportive connections, celebrating your culture, breaking free from labels, and practicing self-acceptance so you can be you, for real.

? Who Am I, Really?

Identity is one of the biggest questions you will ever explore. It is not just about what people see on the outside but also the values, passions, and truths you carry inside. Figuring out who you are takes reflection and practice, and this section helps you explore the puzzle of identity, look beyond labels, notice when you feel most like yourself, and create a picture of the real you.

? Identity Puzzle: Roles, Labels, Passions

Identity has many pieces, and not all of them are chosen by you. Some come from your family, school, culture, or friends, while others come from what you truly enjoy and believe in. Seeing your identity as a puzzle can help you notice which pieces fit and which ones feel out of place. Here's how to work with the puzzle:

- Write down the roles you play in daily life (student, sibling, teammate, friend)
- Add labels you have been given, both positive and negative
- List the passions, hobbies, or causes that make you feel alive
- Notice which pieces belong to you and which feel forced

When you step back and look at the whole puzzle, you see that no single piece defines you. The bigger picture is always more powerful than one role or label.

Authenticity is the foundation of true welbeing.

What Makes You You Beyond What Others Say

People often try to tell you who you are, but their words do not capture your full story. Your real identity shows up in the moments when you live in line with your own values and strengths. Exploring this side of yourself helps you take ownership of who you are becoming. Consider these prompts:

- What three qualities do you admire in yourself?
- When have you felt proud of something that no one else noticed?
- Which values guide your choices, even when they are hard?
- What activities feel like they bring out the truest version of you?

Answering with honesty shows you that your identity is deeper than surface labels. You become more grounded when you choose what defines you instead of letting others decide.

Journal: "I Feel Most Like Myself When...

Journaling can be a mirror that shows you your true self. When you write without judgment, you capture moments where your real identity shines through. This practice helps you spot patterns and reminds you of the situations, people, and places that let you be your authentic self.

Use this journal prompt:

- "I feel most like myself when..." and finish the sentence as many times as you can
- Write about times when you felt free, accepted, or at peace
- Notice what environments or activities made it possible
- Highlight themes that show up again and again

Journaling helps you notice your authentic self hiding in everyday moments. Once you see those patterns, you can seek out more of what makes you feel most like you.

Did You Know?

Your brain feels calmer when your actions match your values. Neuroscience research shows that when people live in line with their true self, their stress response lowers, and they report higher life satisfaction. This means every time you make choices that reflect who you really are, you are literally supporting your mental health.

Make an "I Am" Collage

A collage can capture identity in a creative way that words sometimes cannot. By gathering images, colors, and words that reflect who you are, you give yourself a visual reminder of your strengths and passions. This activity lets you see your identity come alive on paper.

Build your collage like this:

- Collect pictures from magazines, printouts, or drawings
- Add words or quotes that inspire you
- Use symbols for your hobbies, values, and dreams
- Arrange them in a way that feels meaningful to you

When you finish, you will have a visual snapshot of your authentic self. Your collage becomes a reminder that you are made of many layers, and each one is worth celebrating.

Finding Your People

Belonging is more than just fitting in. It is about being surrounded by people who see you, respect you, and accept you as you are. Real connection helps you feel safe enough to grow, take risks, and share your true self. I have noticed that when I am with the right people, I feel lighter and more confident, and that is the power of belonging. This section explores what belonging feels like, how to spot groups that lift you up or drag you down, and how to map your circle of connection.

🧑‍🤝‍🧑What Real Belonging Feels Like

Belonging is not about pretending to fit into a group. It is about feeling safe enough to be yourself without fear of rejection. When you belong, you feel accepted, supported, and valued in a way that makes you stronger. Notice the signs of belonging:

- You can relax and just be yourself
- You feel included, not pressured to change
- People listen and respect your opinions
- You feel lighter after spending time with them

When you find this feeling, it strengthens your confidence. Real belonging reminds you that you do not have to hide who you are to be loved and accepted.

⚖️ Signs of Supportive vs. Draining Groups

Not every group is good for you. Some relationships fill you with energy, while others leave you tired or insecure. Learning to notice this difference helps you make better choices about who you give your time to. Compare these signs:

- Supportive groups cheer for your growth
- They respect your boundaries
- You feel safe sharing your feelings

Choosing supportive groups allows you to grow stronger. You deserve to be surrounded by people who build you up, not those who pull you down.

🔘 Circle of Connection Drawing

Seeing your relationships visually can help you understand where you feel closest and where you feel distant. It also gives you a clear picture of who brings comfort and who adds stress. A circle of connection drawing is a simple way to map this out. Here is how to try it:

- Draw a circle and place yourself in the center
- Add names of people you feel close to near the center
- Place people you feel less connected to farther out
- Notice who makes you feel safe and who drains your energy

Looking at your circle helps you see which relationships support you most. It also shows where you may want to build new connections.

🏠 Spaces Where You Feel Safe to Be Real

Certain spaces allow you to drop the mask and just be yourself. They give you a sense of comfort that makes it easier to breathe and relax. These safe spaces matter because they remind you that you do not have to change to belong.

Think of examples like:

- A best friend's house
- A club or sports team that values you
- Online spaces where you connect with supportive people
- Family gatherings where you feel understood

Identify where you feel most authentic and make time for those spaces. They remind you that being yourself is enough and that you deserve to be in places where you feel safe.

🌍 Culture, Community, and Pride

Your culture and community are an important part of who you are. They shape the way you see the world, the traditions you carry, and the values you live by. I have found strength in my own roots, and you can too. This section explores how to celebrate what makes your background unique, connect with the stories of your family or community, and build pride in your identity.

⚡ Fun Fact

Loneliness can increase stress hormones like cortisol, while real belonging boosts oxytocin, the bonding hormone. That is why being around people who accept you does more than feel good emotionally; it strengthens your body and brain, too. Supportive friendships are not just nice to have; they are part of your health.

🎉 Celebrate What Makes Your Background Unique

Your background holds stories, traditions, and experiences that make you who you are. Sometimes it is easy to forget that what feels ordinary to you is actually something special. By celebrating what makes your background unique, you recognize the strength and richness you carry.

Ways to celebrate include:

- Write down traditions or rituals that matter to you
- Share a favorite meal or recipe from your culture
- Teach a friend about a saying or belief you value
- Collect objects or photos that represent your roots

When you honor your uniqueness, you remind yourself that there is no single way to be "enough." Your background is part of your power, not something to hide.

🎤 Interview Someone in Your Family or Community

The people in your family or community often carry wisdom and stories that can guide you. Taking the time to ask questions helps you connect to where you come from and the resilience of those before you. These stories often bring perspective and pride. Try this approach:

- Ask about challenges they overcame
- Learn about the traditions or values they held onto
- Write down their answers in a journal
- Reflect on how their story connects with your own

Hearing real experiences gives you a sense of continuity and strength. It reminds you that you come from people who faced challenges and still kept going. Their story can inspire you to keep moving forward with courage.

Create a Cultural Strength Shield

A cultural strength shield is a fun, creative way to represent the strengths you inherit from your background. It lets you see your culture as a source of protection and pride instead of something you take for granted. Here's how to make one:

- Draw a shield divided into four parts
- In each section, write or draw one cultural strength
- Examples: courage, family bonds, creativity, resilience
- Decorate your shield with symbols, colors, or words that matter to you

When you finish, place your shield where you can see it. Each time you look at it, you will be reminded that your roots give you strength, even on days when you doubt yourself.

My Roots, My Values Activity

Your roots influence your values, whether through family traditions, cultural beliefs, or community experiences. Taking time to name those values helps you see what guides your decisions and what gives you meaning. Try this reflection:

- Write down three values you learned from your roots
- Note how each one shows up in your life today
- Ask yourself: which values do I want to keep carrying forward?

- Create a statement: "My roots taught me to value ____________, and I live this by ____________."

When you honor your values, you build a foundation for who you are becoming. Your roots give you a sense of identity, and your values show you the direction you want to go.

Topic	Key Idea	How to Practice
When Labels Help vs. Limit	Labels can guide or trap you. Helpful ones support, limiting ones shrink.	Notice how labels affect you, keep what empowers, release what confines.
Rewrite the Labels	You don't have to accept labels given by others.	Write down old labels, cross out false ones, rewrite with empowering words (e.g., "shy" → "thoughtful").
"I'm More Than Just..." Journal	Labels can't capture your full identity.	Write "I'm more than just..." and list endings. See your many roles and strengths.
Make Your Own Label	Create labels with pride instead of accepting imposed ones.	Pick a word or phrase that feels true, decorate it, and display it as a reminder.

Being You Out Loud

To be yourself in a world that is constantly trying to make you something else is the greatest accomplishment.
-Ralph Waldo Emerson

Being yourself is not just about knowing who you are; it is about having the courage to live it. I used to hold back parts of myself out of fear of judgment, but that only made me feel smaller. When you accept yourself and express who you are, you feel lighter and more connected to others. This section explores how to practice self-acceptance, use affirmations, celebrate your quirks, and recognize role models who inspire you to live authentically. You deserve to take up space as your real self.

💖 Practicing Self-Acceptance

Self-acceptance means choosing to value yourself as you are, even when you are not perfect. It does not mean ignoring growth; it means treating yourself with kindness while you grow. Ways to practice self-acceptance:

- Notice when you are being hard on yourself and soften your words
- Remind yourself that mistakes are part of being human
- Focus on your strengths as much as your struggles
- Let yourself take pride in small progress

When you accept yourself, you build the foundation for confidence. It becomes easier to show up authentically because you are no longer hiding behind self-criticism.

Affirmations for Showing Up as Yourself

Affirmations are simple, positive statements that help you believe in yourself. Repeating them regularly strengthens your mindset and makes it easier to show up as your real self.

Try saying these affirmations:

- "I am enough just as I am."
- "My voice matters, and my presence counts."
- "I do not need to be perfect to be worthy."
- "I can show up as me, and that is enough."

Repeat them in the mirror, write them in your journal, or set them as reminders on your phone. Affirmations help quiet doubt and remind you of your worth every single day.

Celebrate Your Quirks Challenge

Your quirks are the unique traits that make you different from everyone else. Instead of hiding them, you can celebrate them. They are part of what makes you special.

Here is a challenge:

- List three quirks you have that make you unique
- Think about how these quirks add to your personality
- Share one with a trusted friend and own it with pride
- Try to notice the quirks in others and celebrate them too

When you celebrate quirks, you turn what once felt like flaws into strengths. You embrace what makes you stand out and inspire others to do the same.

Role Model Shout-Out

Sometimes, it helps to look at people who live authentically and learn from their example. Role models show you what it looks like to be yourself with confidence.

Here is how to do a role model shout-out:

- Pick someone you admire for being real and authentic
- Write down what you appreciate about them
- Share with them if possible, or keep it as a reminder for yourself
- Ask, "How can I bring more of that energy into my own life?"

Recognizing role models reminds you that being yourself is powerful. It gives you permission to express your own truth without apology.

🧥 Story Time: The Hoodie That Didn't Fit

In middle school, I bought a hoodie just because everyone else had the same one. I wore it every day, thinking it would help me fit in. The truth was, I never felt comfortable in it. I still remember the first day I left it at home and wore something I actually liked. To my surprise, no one cared, and a friend even said, "That looks more like you." That moment taught me something important: trying to fit in only made me smaller, but showing up as myself made me feel lighter. Belonging started when I stopped hiding.

🧭 Living the Life You Want

Life is not about waiting for the perfect moment—it is about shaping each day in ways that reflect who you are and what matters most. Living with intention takes practice, courage, and small daily choices. When you know your values and design your days with purpose, you create a life that feels meaningful and truly your own.

🧠 Values: Your Compass for Living

Values are the anchors that guide your choices, relationships, and goals. When you live by them, decisions feel clearer and more peaceful. Reflecting on what makes you proud, sorting your priorities, and naming your top five values turns your inner compass into something visible and reliable. These values become your North Star, helping you stay steady even when life feels confusing.

📅 Designing Your Days With Purpose

The way you spend your time shapes the kind of life you live. By imagining your ideal day, tracking where your energy goes, and aligning your schedule with your values, you begin to take back control of your time. Small changes—like adding one value-driven habit or cutting out energy drains—can turn ordinary days into ones that feel more intentional and fulfilling.

⚖️ Finding Balance Before Burnout

Balance is not about doing everything. It is about creating a rhythm that leaves space for rest, joy, and focus. Learning to recognize the signs of doing too much, practicing guilt-free rest, and making a weekly recharge plan keeps you steady. Saying no with kindness protects your energy so you can say yes to what truly matters.

📚 Keep Growing, Keep Learning

Growth does not come from perfection but from staying open to new lessons. A growth mindset helps you see mistakes as opportunities rather than failures. By celebrating past challenges you have overcome, trying new experiences, and listing the lessons life has already taught you, you remind yourself that you are capable of adapting and expanding. Every step outside your comfort zone rewires your brain for resilience.

🎨 Your Personal Life Toolkit

Life feels more manageable when you have tools to lean on. These may include calming practices, supportive people, affirmations, or daily habits that keep you grounded. Building a "go-to" guide, choosing small routines that support your mind and body, and even writing a letter to your future self, gives you a sense of preparation and strength. Your toolkit is proof that you already hold resources for handling what comes next.

The Heart of Living Intentionally

The life you want is not built overnight. It grows from aligning your choices with your values, designing your time with purpose, caring for your energy, and staying open to growth. It comes from weaving together small, steady actions into a rhythm that reflects who you truly are. The future depends on what you do today, and each choice you make becomes a brick in the foundation of the life you are creating.

📌 Chapter Wrap-Up

Identity is not about changing to fit in; it is about showing up as your real self. In this chapter, you explored the puzzle of identity, noticed what makes you authentic, and practiced celebrating your roots and values. You discovered that true belonging comes from supportive connections and safe spaces. You also learned how to break free from limiting labels, create your own empowering ones, and practice self-acceptance. Being yourself is the strongest way to belong.

🏠 Parents' Corner: Let's Think Together

Activity: Where Do You Feel Most Yourself?

Spend 20 minutes together reflecting on safe spaces. Ask each person to share:

- A place or group where they feel free to be themselves
- One quality they wish others would notice more about them
- Keep it judgment-free, focusing on listening and understanding.

Support Your Teen By:

- Sharing your own stories of feeling pressure to fit in
- Affirming their quirks and unique qualities out loud
- Celebrating family traditions, culture, and roots together
- Respecting their voice when they say who they are becoming
- Modeling self-acceptance instead of self-criticism

When teens see belonging practiced at home, they carry that confidence into friendships, school, and future communities.

Key Takeaways

- Identity is made of many pieces, not just labels or roles.
- Real belonging happens when you feel safe to be yourself.
- Supportive groups lift you up, while draining ones pull you down.
- Your culture, roots, and values are sources of strength.
- You can rewrite limiting labels and choose new ones with pride.
- Practicing self-acceptance helps you live authentically and confidently into friendships, school, and future communities.

Exercise 1: Red Flag vs. Green Flag

Make two lists: red flags in friendships (warning signs) and green flags (positive signs).

Red Flags (warning signs):

____

____

____

____

____

____

____

Green Flags (positive signs):

____

____

____

____

____

____

____

Exercise 2: Kindness Check

Do one kind thing for a friend this week. Write about how it felt for you and how it seemed to feel for them.

What I Did:

How It Felt for Me:

How It Felt for Them (what I noticed):

CONCLUSION

Living the Life You Want

> ***"Life isn't about finding yourself, it's about creating yourself."***
>
> **– George Bernard Shaw**

REACHING THE END of this book does not mean your journey is finished. It means you are stepping into a new beginning with tools, insights, and confidence that you may not have had before. Along the way, you have faced difficult questions, explored your emotions, and practiced skills to help you feel more in control of your life. These pages were never about making you perfect. They were about showing you that you already have the strength to keep moving forward, even when life feels heavy.

You now understand that thoughts, feelings, and actions are deeply connected. When one shifts, the others often follow. This is the core of Cognitive Behavioral Therapy, and it is something you can carry with you into every stage of life. The small steps you take each day matter. With time, they shape how you see yourself, how you respond to challenges, and how much peace you allow into your life.

Confidence has never been about being fearless. It has always been about showing up anyway, even when fear is present. Anxiety is not proof that you are weak or broken. It is proof that you are human, with a mind that tries to protect you, even if sometimes it works too hard.

Resting when you are tired is not weakness but wisdom. Speaking to yourself with kindness builds resilience in a way that criticism never could. Asking for help is not failure but a choice to lean on the strength of others when your own feels stretched thin. And peace is not something you wait to feel someday when life finally calms down. It can begin here, in the choices you make today.

One of the biggest lessons you have uncovered is the power of small steps. Progress does not come from waiting for the perfect moment. It comes from everyday choices that seem small but carry weight. Taking one deep breath before reacting, reaching out to a friend when you want to shut down, writing down one win in your journal, or choosing rest when exhaustion creeps in may not feel like major victories, but they are the building blocks of a steadier, stronger life. With time, they add up and become the foundation of confidence.

You also carry with you a personal toolkit. This toolkit is made up of grounding skills, coping strategies, and reminders of strength you practiced in these chapters. It is yours to use whenever life feels uncertain. You can revisit your calm kit, write in your journal when your thoughts feel too heavy, return to your breathing exercises, or reread reflections that remind you of how far you have come. Your toolkit is not fixed. It grows with you. Each time you discover a new strategy or add a new reminder, it becomes stronger, just as you do.

Of course, storms will still come. No book, no set of tools, and no amount of practice can prevent the hard parts of life. But you now know that storms pass. You know that you can steady yourself while you walk through them. You know that you can pause, breathe, lean on someone who cares, and choose how you respond. When the next storm arrives, you can remind yourself that you have already faced hard times and made it through. You can tell yourself that this moment will not last forever. You can remember that even in struggle, you are never truly alone.

The choices you make from here will shape the life you live. Confidence and peace are not waiting in the future. They are created in how you speak to yourself, in how you show up when life feels unfair, and in how you rise after setbacks. Asking yourself what matters most, aligning your choices with your values, creating space for calm in your day, and taking even the smallest step toward what you want will keep guiding you toward a life that feels real and meaningful.

It is also important to remember that you are not alone. You have people who care about you, and you have yourself. Both are sources of strength. Reaching out when you need support is courage, not weakness. Trusting yourself is not selfish but necessary. Whenever you begin to doubt your worth, you can return to the truths you have practiced here: no feeling lasts forever, small steps count, you are capable of more than you believe, and peace is possible even in the middle of struggle.

This book was never about erasing anxiety or pretending life is easy. It was about helping you see that you already have the tools to handle the difficult moments and to build more joyful ones. From here, the path is yours to walk. You may choose to revisit some of the chapters, share what you have learned with a friend, or start a new ritual that gives your days more calm. However you continue, it does not need to be perfect. It only needs to be yours.

You are not defined by fear, stress, or self-doubt. You are defined by your persistence, your growth, and your willingness to keep showing up. Every time you take a step forward, no matter how small, you are proving to yourself that you are stronger than you once believed.

Carry this truth with you: you are enough exactly as you are, and you have the power to live the life you want.

Congratulations!
You've won a
BONUS BOOK

You did it!

YOU'VE REACHED THE END OF THE BOOK...

but the adventure doesn't have to stop here.

As a special thank-you for BEING SUCH an awesome reader, you get exclusive access to a FREE bonus book... just for finishing this one.

Your Bonus Adventure is Waiting.

👉 How to Get Your PDF:

1. Go to *www.*emmadavisbooks.com/freegift
2. Sign in using your ***email address***.
3. Enter the ***unique code*** for your book.
4. Download your f***ree PDF workbook*** instantly.

Use this code for your **free book**:

9S2A7V4K

Please leave a
Review

Hi, can you help us out?
If you enjoyed this book, please take a moment to leave a review at:

emmadavisbooks.com
or
Amazon.com

SCAN ME

Your review helps us reach more teens and the people who care about them—and keeps us inspired to create more books for you.
Thank you for your support!

ABOUT THE AUTHOR

Emma Davis is a woman who wears many hats. She is a clinical social worker, a therapist, and a financial advisor, as well as the author of Effective Anger Management for Teens.

Her books are aimed at teenagers, covering a diverse range of topics, including life and coping skills, DBT techniques, finances, puberty, developing a growth mindset, and career planning. She focuses on the unique challenges faced by adolescents in their emotional and physiological development, empowering readers with a strong foundation for understanding.

Emma draws on experience and knowledge from all her roles, as well as her experience as a mother, to guide young people through the difficult stage of adolescence. She runs a therapy practice and financial education agency tailored to teenagers, and has worked with a diverse range of young people facing different practical and emotional challenges. She also runs several online courses on cultivating interpersonal skills, gratitude, happiness, and joy, as well as 10 residential care facilities for adults with disabilities and mental health challenges, which also informs her work.

Emma is married with 9 children between the ages of 3 and 22. She enjoys spending time with her family, practicing jiu jitsu, and developing her skills in photography.

Additional Resources

Hotlines & Text Lines

- **988 Suicide & Crisis Lifeline (U.S.)** – Call or text 988, 24/7 support
- **Crisis Text Line** – Text **HOME** to 741741 (U.S./Canada), free and confidential
- **Teen Line** – Call **1-800-852-8336** or text **TEEN** (839863), peer support for teens
- **Kids Help Phone (Canada)** – Call **1-800-668-6868** or text **CONNECT** to 686868

CBT-Friendly Websites

- **ReachOut.com** – Articles, tools, and real stories from teens
- **GetSelfHelp.co.uk** – Free CBT worksheets and thought-challenging exercises
- **MoodGym** – Interactive CBT-based activities and coping tools

Apps Based on CBT

- **MindShift CBT** – Helps with anxiety using CBT tools and coping strategies
- **Woebot** – Chat-based CBT support with daily mood check-ins
- **Sanvello** – CBT tools, mood tracking, and guided thought exercises
- **Youper** – AI journal to challenge thoughts and reframe stressors

Helpful Books / Workbooks

- ***The Body Keeps the Score* by Bessel van der Kolk**
  Explores how trauma reshapes the body and brain, and offers innovative treatments beyond traditional talk therapy.

- *Lost Connections* **by Johann Hari**
  Investigates the root causes of depression and anxiety, emphasizing the importance of connection and purpose in healing.
- *Feeling Good: The New Mood Therapy* **by Dr. David D. Burns**
  A practical guide based on cognitive-behavioral therapy (CBT) techniques to combat negative thoughts and improve mood.

Helping Teens With Finances,
Anger Management, Mental Health,
And Future Life Planning

From

EMMA DAVIS

Available on Amazon
or wherever books are sold

To learn more about helping teens with finances, anger management, mental health, and future life planning please join my newsletter! at www.emmadavisbooks.com

BIBLIOGRAPHY

Aldao, A., Nolen-Hoeksema, S., & Schweizer, S. (2010). Emotion-regulation strategies across psychopathology: A meta-analytic review. *Clinical Psychology Review*, 30(2), 217–237. https://doi.org/10.1016/j.cpr.2009.11.004

Berg, M., Lindegaard, T., Flygare, A., Sjöbrink, J., Hagvall, L., Palmebäck, S., ... & Andersson, G. (2022). Internet-based CBT for adolescents with low self-esteem: A pilot randomized controlled trial. *Cognitive Behaviour Therapy*, 51(5), 388–407. https://doi.org/10.1080/16506073.2022.2060856

Bluth, K., & Eisenlohr-Moul, T. A. (2017). Response to stress in adolescents: Self-compassion and self-criticism. *Journal of Adolescence*, 57, 120–128. https://doi.org/10.1016/j.adolescence.2017.04.001

Butler, A. C., Chapman, J. E., Forman, E. M., & Beck, A. T. (2006). The empirical status of cognitive-behavioral therapy: A review of meta-analyses. *Clinical Psychology Review*, 26(1), 17–31.

Creswell, J. D., Lam, S., Stanton, A. L., Taylor, S. E., Bower, J. E., & Sherman, D. K. (2005). Does self-affirmation improve problem-solving under stress? *Psychological Science*, 16(11), 846–851. https://doi.org/10.1111/j.1467-9280.2005.01624.x

DeRubeis, R. J., Siegle, G. J., & Hollon, S. D. (2008). Cognitive therapy versus medication for depression: Treatment outcomes and neural mechanisms. *Nature Reviews Neuroscience*, 9(10), 788–796. https://doi.org/10.1038/nrn2345

Dunning, D. L., Griffiths, K., Kuyken, W., Crane, C., Foulkes, L., Parker, J., & Dalgleish, T. (2019). Research Review: The effects of mindfulness-based interventions on cognition and mental health in children and adolescents – a meta-analysis of randomized controlled trials. *Journal of Child Psychology and Psychiatry, 60*(3), 244–258. https://doi.org/10.1111/jcpp.12980

Ehret, A. M., Joormann, J., & Berking, M. (2015). Examining self-help strategies in adolescence: The role of positive self-statements in emotional regulation. *Cognitive Therapy and Research, 39*(5), 692–703. https://doi.org/10.1007/s10608-015-9707-2

Ford, B. Q., Lam, P., John, O. P., & Mauss, I. B. (2017). The psychological health benefits of accepting negative emotions and thoughts: Laboratory, diary, and longitudinal evidence. *Journal of Personality and Social Psychology, 113*(3), 329–352. https://doi.org/10.1037/pspp0000132

Frison, E., & Eggermont, S. (2016). Exploring the relationships between different types of Facebook use, perceived online social support, and adolescents' depressed mood. *Social Science Computer Review, 34*(2), 153–171. https://doi.org/10.1177/0894439314567449

Garnefski, N., & Kraaij, V. (2018). Cognitive coping and emotional problems in adolescents. *Journal of Adolescence, 67*, 1–7. https://doi.org/10.1016/j.adolescence.2018.04.002

Hirsch, C. R., Perman, G., Hayes, S., Eagle, R., Baidoo, K., & Jopling, E. (2014). Deliberate versus spontaneous imagery in generalized anxiety disorder: Using guided imagery to investigate self-image. *Behaviour Research and Therapy, 57*, 8–15.

Hofmann, S. G., Asnaani, A., Vonk, I. J. J., Sawyer, A. T., & Fang, A. (2012). The efficacy of cognitive behavioral therapy: A review of meta-analyses. *Cognitive Therapy and Research, 36*(5), 427–440. https://doi.org/10.1007/s10608-012-9476-1

Kendall, P. C., et al. (2016). The effects of cognitive restructuring in CBT for anxious youth. *Journal of Child Psychology and Psychiatry, 57*(3), 233–241. https://doi.org/10.1111/jcpp.12461

Kuyken, W., Byford, S., Taylor, R. S., Watkins, E., Holden, E., White, K., Barrett, B., Byng, R., Evans, A., & Teasdale, J. D. (2010).

Mindfulness-based cognitive therapy to prevent relapse in adolescents with recurrent depression: A randomized controlled trial. *Journal of Adolescence, 33*(1), 45–55. https://doi.org/10.1016/j.adolescence.2009.06.003

Masuda, A., Hayes, S. C., Sackett, C. F., & Twohig, M. P. (2004). Cognitive defusion and self-relevant negative thoughts: Examining the impact of a ninety-year-old technique. *Behaviour Research and Therapy, 42*(4), 477–485. https://doi.org/10.1016/S0005-7967(03)00143-6

Meier, A., & Reinecke, L. (2020). Computer-mediated communication, social media, and mental health: A conceptual and empirical meta-review. *Communication Research, 47*(8), 1167–1201. https://doi.org/10.1177/0093650219826000

Metzler, H., Vilarem, E., Petschen, A., & Grèzes, J. (2023). Power pose effects on approach and avoidance decisions in response to social threat. *PLOS ONE, 18*(8), e0286904. https://doi.org/10.1371/journal.pone.0286904

National Institute for Health and Care Excellence (NICE). (2019).

Neff, K. D., & McGehee, P. (2010). Self-compassion and psychological resilience among adolescents and young adults. *Self and Identity, 9*(3), 225–240. https://doi.org/10.1080/15298860902979307

Nesi, J., & Prinstein, M. J. (2015). Using social media for social comparison and feedback-seeking: Gender and popularity moderate associations with depressive symptoms. *Journal of Abnormal Child Psychology, 43*(8), 1427–1438. https://doi.org/10.1007/s10802-015-0020-0

Ouellette, J. A., & Wood, W. (1998). Habit and intention in everyday life: The multiple processes by which past behavior predicts future behavior. *Psychological Bulletin, 124*(1), 54–74. https://doi.org/10.1037/0033-2909.124.1.54

Saarikallio, S. (2011). Music as emotional self-regulation throughout adulthood. *Psychology of Music, 39*(3), 307–327. https://doi.org/10.1177/0305735610374894

Siegle, G. J., Thompson, W., Carter, C. S., Steinhauer, S. R., & Thase, M. E. (2007). Increased amygdala and decreased dorsolateral prefrontal BOLD responses in unipolar depression: Related and independent features. *Biological Psychiatry, 61*(2), 198–209. https://doi.org/10.1016/j.biopsych.2006.05.048

Southam-Gerow, M. A., & Kendall, P. C. (2002). Emotion regulation and understanding: Implications for child psychopathology and therapy. In M. A. Southam-Gerow (Ed.), *Emotion Regulation in Children and Adolescents: A Practitioner's Guide* (pp. 13–38). Guilford Press.

Stallard, P., Richardson, T., Velleman, S., & Attwood, M. (2011). Computerized CBT (Think, Feel, Do) for depression and anxiety in children and adolescents: Outcomes and feedback from a pilot randomized controlled trial. *Behavioural and Cognitive Psychotherapy, 39*(3), 273–284. https://doi.org/10.1017/S135246581000086X

Swee, M. B., Klein, K., Murray, S., & Heimberg, R. G. (2023). A brief self-compassionate letter-writing intervention for individuals with high shame. *Mindfulness, 14*(4), 854–867.

Tandon, P. S., Zhou, C., Johnson, A. M., Gonzalez, E. S., Kroshus, E., & Christakis, D. A. (2022). Associations between screen time and mental health among adolescents during the COVID-19 pandemic. *Journal of Adolescence, 94*, 100–108. https://doi.org/10.1016/j.adolescence.2021.11.005

Teasdale, J. D., Segal, Z. V., Williams, J. M. G., Ridgeway, V. A., Soulsby, J. M., & Lau, M. A. (2000). Prevention of relapse/recurrence in major depression by mindfulness-based cognitive therapy. *Journal of Consulting and Clinical Psychology, 68*(4), 615–623. https://doi.org/10.1037/0022-006X.68.4.615

Urken, D., & LeCroy, C. W. (2021). A randomized controlled trial of a self-compassion writing intervention for adults with mental illness. *Research on Social Work Practice, 31*(3), 254–266. https://doi.org/10.1177/1049731520968455

Verstraeten, K., Bijttebier, P., Vasey, M. W., & Raes, F. (2010). The impact of rumination on adolescents' depressive mood: The role of perceived parenting and school life. *Journal of Abnormal Child Psychology, 38*(6), 701–714.

Vujanovic, A. A., Niles, B. L., Pietrefesa, A. S., Schmertz, S. K., & Potter, C. M. (2011). Mindfulness in the treatment of young adults with anxiety disorders: A replication and extension study. *Behavior Therapy, 42*(1), 204–215. https://doi.org/10.1016/j.beth.2010.05.004

Wilcockson, T. D., Ellis, D. A., & Shaw, H. (2020). Examining the impact of a digital detox on anxiety and depression in adolescents. *Cyberpsychology, Behavior, and Social Networking, 23*(7), 500–505. https://doi.org/10.1089/cyber.2019.0496

Yang, C., & Liu, D. (2021). Instagram use and self-esteem: The moderating role of perceived social support. *Cyberpsychology: Journal of Psychosocial Research on Cyberspace, 15*(1), Article 2. https://doi.org/10.5817/CP2021-1-2

Zoogman, S., Goldberg, S. B., Hoyt, W. T., & Miller, L. (2015). Mindfulness interventions with youth: A meta-analysis. *Mindfulness, 6*(2), 290–302. https://doi.org/10.1007/s12671-013-0260-4

Made in United States
North Haven, CT
02 September 2026

17862380R00108